HAROLD B. LEE

Harold Bingham Lee

HAROLD B. LEE

LIFE AND THOUGHT

NEWELL G. BRINGHURST

SIGNATURE BOOKS | 2021 | SALT LAKE CITY

An index is available on the
Harold B. Lee: Life and Thought page at signaturebooks.com

Design by Jason Francis.

FIRST EDITION | 2021

LIBRARY OF CONGRESS CATALOGING-IN-PUBLICATION DATA

Names: Bringhurst, Newell G., author.

Title: Harold B. Lee : life and thought / Newell G. Bringhurst.

Description: First edition. | Salt Lake City : Signature Books, 2021. | Summary: "While Harold B. Lee served as president of the Church of Jesus Christ of Latter-day Saints for a mere one and half-years— among the shortest tenure of any church leader—his impact on the modern LDS Church remains among the most profound. Lee implemented the Church Welfare Program, which provided relief to suffering church members during the 1930s Great Depression and continues to impact the lives of church members today. As a high-ranking general authority from 1941 to 1973, he championed other innovations, the most important being Correlation. Lee acted in response to the church's record growth and increased diversity to consolidate and streamline churchwide instruction and administration. As a teacher/mentor, he promoted conservative church doctrine and practice, which influenced a generation of church leaders, including future presidents Spencer W. Kimball, Ezra Taft Benson, Howard W. Hunter, Gordon B. Hinckley, and Thomas S. Monson. Noted historian Newell G. Bringhurst succinctly narrates the major, defining events in Lee's remarkable life, while highlighting Lee's important, lasting contributions" —Provided by publisher.

Identifiers: LCCN 2021039914 (print) | LCCN 2021039915 (ebook) | ISBN 9781560854432 (paperback) | ISBN 9781560854029 (ebook)

Subjects: LCSH: Lee, Harold B., 1899-1973. | Church of Jesus Christ of Latter-day Saints—Presidents—Biography. | Mormons—United States—Biography. | LCGFT: Biographies.

Classification: LCC BX8695.L396 B75 2021 (print) | LCC BX8695.L396 (ebook) | DDC 289.3092 [B]—dc23

LC record available at https://lccn.loc.gov/2021039914
LC ebook record available at https://lccn.loc.gov/2021039915

To members of my close-knit immediate family:
my wife, Mary Ann,
daughter, Laura Alice Bringhurst,
son-in-law, David Isaacs, and
grandsons, Ramsay David and Victor Newell Isaacs.

CONTENTS

ACKNOWLEDGMENTS

A number of individuals and institutions provided invaluable help over the four years during which I labored on this biography.

Special thanks to Gary James Bergera, who encouraged me to undertake this project. He provided continuing encouragement as I moved forward with the research and writing.

Most helpful in providing documentary materials were several libraries: the LDS Church History Library, the University of Utah Special Collections Library, the Utah State University Special Collections Library, and the Brigham Young University Special Collections Library. Special thanks to Craig L. Foster, research associate at the LDS Family History Library, who provided valuable information on Harold Lee and his family not available elsewhere. Likewise, Reid Moon, owner of Moon's Rare Books, in Provo, Utah, allowed me access to a collection of Harold B. Lee's personal correspondence and assorted materials, which provided further family information not available elsewhere.

As I commenced writing, a number of individuals read all and/ or parts of the manuscript, offering suggestions for improvement, including Matthew L. Harris, professor of history, Colorado State University, Pueblo; Craig L. Foster, LDS Family History Library; and Mathew Bowman, Howard W. Hunter Chair of LDS History, Claremont University. Also reading early drafts were members of the Visalia (California) Writers Group: Arthur Neeson, Stewart Wilson, and Janet LeBaron. Gary James Bergera read the final draft and helped to further improve it.

Finally, this volume would not have been possible without the support of my ever-patient wife, Mary Ann, who encouraged me throughout the most stressful time of the COVID-19 pandemic.

All such help notwithstanding, I alone assume responsibility for the biography's accuracy and the contents thereof.

INTRODUCTION

First, the obvious question: Why a new, albeit short, biography of Harold B. Lee? To many members of the Church of Jesus Christ of Latter-day Saints, as well as those outside the faith, Lee is virtually a forgotten figure in the twenty-first century. If recalled at all, it is for the dubious distinction of being among the briefest-serving LDS Church presidents. Lee's tenure as president ended abruptly eighteen months after it began when he died suddenly on December 26, 1973 at age seventy-four.

However, I contend that Lee was among the most important twentieth-century LDS leaders. His impact on the church was considerable over the thirty years that he served as a general authority, initially, as a member of the Quorum of Twelve Apostles, 1941–70; then as first counselor in the First Presidency, 1970–72; and ultimately as church president. Even before that, Lee distinguished himself as the facilitator of the LDS Church Welfare Program, which provided relief for church members suffering from the ravages of the 1930s Great Depression. Following his elevation to the Twelve at age forty-one, Lee further served the church in refining and implementing Correlation—a long-range program to streamline the church's organizational structure and upgrade its various programs and educational curricula. As church president from July 1972 to December 1973, he pushed Correlation forward in response to the church's changing demographics, especially its rapid expansion into an international organization.

All subsequent LDS presidents continued to expand on Lee's pioneering Correlation efforts. Involved in this process were all six of

Lee's successors. Each, moreover, was either a close associate and/or protégé of Lee: Spencer W. Kimball, Ezra Taft Benson, Howard W. Hunter, Gordon B. Hinckley, Thomas S. Monson, and current LDS president Russell M. Nelson.

Given his impact on the development of the modern LDS Church, Lee rightly deserves to be ranked with five other seminal twentieth-century presidents—Heber J. Grant, David O. McKay, Joseph Fielding Smith, Spencer W. Kimball, and Gordon B. Hinckley—all of whom Lee interacted with. Lee was also a close friend of another important church leader, J. Reuben Clark—a longtime counselor in the First Presidency, from 1933 to 1961. Lee, influenced by Clark, championed his mentor's conservative, orthodox agenda concerning church doctrine and beliefs, including priesthood and temple participation denial to black church members, a practice Lee vigorously upheld as doctrine.

I believe Lee deserves a new biography because his central role as the major architect of modern Mormonism has not received sufficient attention in previous studies.

*

Thus, this brief biography focuses on Lee relative to his impact on the Church of Jesus Christ of Latter-day Saints. It further considers Lee's singular, unwavering devotion to church service within the broader context of his life experiences and multi-faceted personality.

Indeed, an understanding of Lee's complex personality provides crucial insights into both the man and his ability to achieve. Among Lee's outstanding qualities was his extreme intelligence, evident from his youth on, and initially reflected in his performance as an outstanding student, talented musician, and skilled athlete. Lee's precocity in all that he undertook caused his father to remark, "We expect big things of you." The dutiful son did not disappoint.

A second, related characteristic was Lee's compulsive, relentless drive to excel. This characteristic was the result of family dynamics combined with an innate, anxious urge to be continuously engaged in some useful activity. Reflective of this characteristic was Lee's "quick action-oriented disposition" which caused him to express impatience with associates whom he deemed as failing to act with sufficient speed in carrying out his mandates.

A third important trait was Lee's "fiery temper"—a characteristic frankly acknowledged by family and close working associates. Those affected by Lee's outbursts usually excused his behavior by conceding that such fits of temper tended to be of short duration and that he did not hold lasting grudges.

*

In researching and writing this biography, I used a variety of published and unpublished sources. By far the most important references on Lee's life are two book-length biographies. The first is *Harold B. Lee: Prophet and Seer*, penned by Lesley Brent Goates—the late Mormon leader's son-in-law—and published by Bookcraft of Salt Lake City in 1985. The second, *Harold B. Lee: Man of Vision, Prophet of God*, published by the Deseret Book Company in 1993, was authored by Francis M. Gibbons—a secretary to the First Presidency during Lee's tenure, a general church authority himself, and the prolific author of biographies of various LDS Church presidents. Goates's biography was sanctioned by the Lee family and is rightly an authorized biography. Gibbons's biography was written by a bureaucracy insider with the full support of the LDS Church and may also be thought of, to a certain extent, as authorized. (Throughout the notes, both biographies are cited simply as Goates or Gibbons, followed by the relevant page numbers.)

Both volumes contain important information drawn from primary sources not readily available elsewhere. In particular, Goates's *Lee* quotes extensively from Lee's personal diaries and other unpublished writings—all of which provide essential, sometimes unparalleled insights into the personality of Lee's "inner man" reacting to the crucial events unfolding around him. Gibbons's *Lee* likewise proved useful in that the author's vividly written narrative skillfully locates the Mormon leader in the context of his time and place, while reflecting the author's personal association with Lee as president.

Also providing important information and insights are the published writings of Lee himself, specifically his sermons, a number of which are contained in *The Teachings of Harold B. Lee* (1996), edited by Clyde J. Williams; and also two volumes, written and edited by Lee, *Decisions for Successful Living* (1973) and *Stand Ye in Holy Places: Selected Sermons and Writings of President Harold B. Lee* (1974). I also consulted two important oral histories by Lee family members: those of his daughter, Helen Lee Goates, and of son-in-law Brent Goates, both of which provided valuable insights into Lee's relationships with family and others close to him. Offering an additional perspective is a collection of Lee's personal correspondence and assorted materials acquired by Utah-based rare book dealer Reid Moon, who kindly allowed access to these important unpublished materials.

CHAPTER ONE

CHILDHOOD AND COMING OF AGE

1899–1916

Harold Bingham Lee, eleventh president of the Church of Jesus Christ of Latter-day Saints, was born on March 28, 1899, in the tiny Mormon town of Clifton, Idaho, where he also came of age.

Clifton, located in southwestern Idaho within the upper Cache Valley, was settled by white Mormon pioneers led by Thomas Charles Howell and his sons in the spring of 1869. As more migrants arrived, a branch of the LDS Church was organized, followed by a fully functioning ward in 1877. The local economy was, and continues to be, dependent on small-scale agriculture—a challenging, precarious occupation given the region's high elevation of 4,852 feet, combined with its relative short growing season and its uncertain, volatile weather. Thus, the number of individuals living there was relatively limited, which remains the case. In 1920 the town's population stood at 234 inhabitants according to US Census figures. By 2018 Clifton's population had grown to 301. Originally a part of Oneida County, Clifton became part of Franklin County in 1913. Clifton is part of the larger Logan, Utah–Idaho metropolitan area.[1]

Besides Harold B. Lee, Clifton boasts at least one other noteworthy native—Tara Westover, author of the best-selling *Educated*, the acclaimed memoir of growing up and coming of age in the same tiny Mormon-dominated community.[2]

*

Harold B. Lee's progenitors were of English–Scottish heritage

---

1. For a brief overview of Clifton, see Andrew Jensen, *Encyclopedic History of the Church of Jesus Christ of Latter-day Saints* (Salt Lake City: Deseret News Press, 1941), 148.
2. Tara Westover, *Educated* (New York: Penguin Random House, 2018).

and boasted a multi-generational Latter-day Saint background. The majority cast their lot with the church from the 1830s through the 1850s. Harold's great-great-grandfather Francis Lee joined the church in 1832—just two years after its founding.[3] The future leader's ancestors were generally middle-echelon, rank-and-file members in terms of economic status and church callings. A notable exception was Joseph William McMurrin—Harold's great-uncle, called to the church's prestigious Council of the Seventy in 1897 and where he served until 1931.[4]

Harold's father, Samuel Marion Lee, was born in Panaca, Nevada, on November 22, 1875. Samuel experienced a precarious, unsettled childhood. Born prematurely, he weighed just three-and-half pounds. Worse still, his mother, Margaret McMurrin Lee, exhausted by the difficult birth, died three days later. Soon thereafter, Samuel was abandoned by his father, Francis Lee, unable and/or unwilling to care for his frail offspring. The elder Lee gave Samuel to his late wife's parents, Joseph and Margaret Leaing McMurrin, who lived in Salt Lake City. Young Samuel experienced additional adversity when his grandfather McMurrin was convicted of unlawful cohabitation and subsequently imprisoned during the 1880s—the result of taking a second wife, Jeanette Irving. Samuel's uncle Joseph W. McMurrin—also a polygamist—likewise suffered during the anti-polygamy raids of the 1880s. Joseph W. was shot twice in the abdomen and nearly died, the result of an aggressive federal officer seeking to arrest him.[5]

By 1893, seventeen-year-old Samuel had come of age and struck out on his own. His grandmother McMurrin, to whom he was extremely close, had died. The bereaved young man took up residence in Clifton, Idaho, at the invitation of his uncle and aunt, Riley and Jeanette McMurrin Davis, who employed him to work on their family farm. Samuel's move to Clifton brought him into contact with Louisa Emeline Bingham, whom he ultimately married.[6]

---

3. For a detailed discussion of Harold B. Lee's immediate ancestors, see Goates, 3–16, and Gibbons, 1–11.

4. Goates, 12–13. Joseph W. McMurrin was the grandfather of Sterling M. McMurrin, making the noted liberal philosopher and critic of Mormon orthodoxy Harold's second cousin.

5. Gibbons, 10.

6. Gibbons, 10.

Louisa Emeline Bingham was the oldest of three children born to Perry Calvin and Rachel Henderson Bingham. Louisa's father, Perry, was a successful freighter and cattle broker who achieved a degree of local prominence. Perry was elected as sheriff and assessor of Oneida County, and subsequently appointed deputy warden of the Idaho State Prison. This latter appointment required him to spend significant time in Boise, where the prison was located. Perry's frequent absences left care of the family up his wife, Rachel. Unfortunately, Rachel suffered from chronic health problems, rendering her incapable of assuming most such responsibilities.[7]

Thus Louisa, as the oldest child, while still a young teenager, took over supervising the household and overseeing her younger siblings while caring for her increasingly invalid mother. Louisa performed a variety of outside chores as well. All of this deprived Louisa of "the luxury of being a child" and compelled her "to mature very fast."[8]

While a teenager, Louisa met and fell in love with Samuel Lee. As their courtship intensified, the couple made plans to marry. But in February 1896, Samuel received a call to serve an LDS mission in the southern United States. Samuel faced the difficult choice of whether to leave Louisa behind for two years of mission service or move forward with their planned wedding.[9]

*

In the end, Samuel chose immediate marriage. Louisa, barely seventeen years old, and twenty-year-old Samuel were married on May 13, 1896, in the LDS Logan Temple by Marriner W. Merrill, temple president and LDS apostle. Despite their youth, Samuel and Louisa found that their earlier difficulties had prepared them for the challenges that lay ahead.[10]

---

7. Gibbons, 10.

8. Quoted in Gibbons, 11. For two additional perspectives on Louisa Emmeline Bingham Lee, see Jaynan M. Payne, "Louisa Emmeline Bingham Lee," and "Louisa B. Lee Dies in S.L. of Heart Ailment," undated obituary, both at www.familysearch.org/photos/artifacts/12718840.

9. As indicated by First Presidency Missionary Calls and Recommendations, 1877–1918, CR 1 168, Church History Library, Church of Jesus Christ of Latter-day Saints, Salt Lake City. This source further indicates that "On 3 February 1896 Samuel M. Lee accepts his call to serve his call to the Southern States to begin 1 May 1896." But in the end, Samuel rescinded his initial acceptance.

10. Gibbons, 11.

Over the fourteen years that followed, Samuel and Louisa became the parents of six children: The first four, all sons, included Samuel Perry, born December 5, 1896; Harold Bingham, born March 28, 1899; Clyde Bingham, October 12, 1902; and finally, Waldo Bingham, November 24, 1905. Their final two children, both daughters, were Stella Bingham, born December 23, 1907, and Verda Bingham, July 1, 1910.

Samuel and Louisa each possessed distinctive attitudes and patterns of behavior that helped to shape Harold's own personality and beliefs. Samuel exhibited a generally "quiet, gentle, compassionate, unassuming" personality unlike that of his famous son. But at the same time, he possessed a strong work ethic, embracing as his dictum: "All individuals are placed on this earth to 'work out our salvation,' with the emphasis on work."[11] This, in turn, inspired Harold who likewise adhered to the concept that one must always be anxiously engaged in some productive activity—a hallmark of his personality over the course of his life.

Samuel likewise passed on to his son an unwavering commitment to the LDS faith. Samuel's strong beliefs stemmed in large measure from the fact that he was a "miracle child," having survived a difficult birth in which his mother perished. Samuel devoutly embraced essential LDS doctrines and beliefs in their entirety. This, in turn, led to his acceptance of a series of church callings, each of increasing responsibility. He served five years as the Clifton Ward's Sunday school superintendent. Following that, he was called as a counselor in the ward bishopric, and was ultimately elevated to the position of bishop—in which capacity he served nine years. As bishop, Samuel acted "as a devoted shepherd of his flock, attending to the temporal and spiritual needs of the widows and others ... who required special attention."[12] A further aspect of Samuel's faith was his avid interest in genealogy, in particular, his "preoccupation with his family lineage." He compiled some "1,500 sheets of family genealogical records."[13] Harold inherited a similar fascination with lineage, which undoubtedly shaped his attitudes on race and ethnicity.

---

11. Gibbons, 11.
12. Gibbons, 15.
13. Goates, 19–20; Gibbons, 14.

Harold's mother, Louisa, through her own strong Mormon beliefs, likewise influenced her son. Louisa, like her husband, was active
in the Clifton Ward, fulfilling a number of church callings. She was
particularly active in the ward's Young Women's Mutual Improvement Association (YWMIA), in which she served as a counselor
and later as president. From there she became second counselor in
the Oneida Stake YWMIA. Louisa also involved herself in the ward
Primary and Relief Society.[14]

Louisa possessed a deep sense of spirituality; she "was prayerful
by nature and frequently offered special, secret prayers for the welfare of her family." Louisa's "habit of prayerfulness [as] an innate
spiritual sense ... prompted her to act instinctively when members
of her family were in peril."[15] In one instance, during an electrical
storm, she suddenly, and for no apparent reason, pushed young Harold out of the doorway of the family house. Soon thereafter, a bolt
of lightning flashed down the chimney and out through the door
where Harold had been standing, leaving "a huge gash in a tree that
stood in the yard." As Harold himself recalled years later, had "I remained in the door opening I would not be [here] today." "My life,"
he added, "was spared because of her impulsive, intuitive nature."[16]

Among Louisa's other qualities was her "extraordinary will-power"
evident in her determination to excel in each and every domestic
pursuit. As a skilled seamstress, Louisa reportedly "could create mas-
terpieces of clothing, and home decorations with a flair."[17] All of her
children's attire had been crafted from "second hand clothes."[18] Her
boys' suits, for example, "had all the latest Lord Fauntleroy ruffles
and trims, very fashionable for the day."[19] Louisa moreover "cooked
with a gourmet touch" a variety of soups and baked goods, according
to daughters Verda and Stella.[20] Also "gifted in the art of flower
arranging ... her [mother's] beautiful handiwork bore the stamp of

---

14. Goates, 24.
15. Gibbons, 16.
16. Quoted in Goates, 41.
17. Payne, "Louisa Emmeline Bingham Lee."
18. Recalled by Harold B. Lee, in Goates, 24.
19. Payne, "Louisa Emmeline Bingham Lee."
20. Quoted in Goates, 25.

her personality in our home."[21] In general, she was an immaculate housekeeper, her home neat and orderly. This caused her husband to remark, "Mother, I do believe that you make dirt just because you enjoy cleaning it up so much."[22]

In addition, Louisa possessed skills in nursing and midwifery, and was often called on to comfort the sick or to preside over the delivery of a baby. She used her healing arts in aid of her own family, specifically many of the well-known home remedies of the day. Young Harold directly benefited from his mother's nursing skills. On one occasion when he lay gravely ill with pneumonia, Louisa initially sought to reduce her son's congestion and lower his fever by applying a series of mustard plasters, which did nothing but turn his chest red. She then sliced an apronful of onions into a boiling pan of water, strained out the water, and placed the onion mass on his chest. Then she prayed. By morning he was breathing much easier and was ultimately healed. On a second occasion, when Harold accidently spilled soap-making lye on his head, face, and arms, Louisa immediately kicked open a large container of beet pickles and splashed the vinegar liquid all over her son, neutralizing the lye and preventing scarring.[23]

Harold inherited yet another important quality from his mother—her blunt frankness. Louisa was uninhibited in speaking her mind. "She spoke openly in words not to be misunderstood. ... It was never necessary to wonder about [her] meaning or about how she stood in her estimation." Likewise, Harold, in the words of a biographer, "was forthright in all his conversations and dealings. He left no room for speculation about what he meant or how he felt."[24]

In summing up his mother, Harold mused: "She was intensely loyal to her friends and equally vindictive toward her enemies. While never unreasonably upholding her family, she would defend them to her death against slander."[25]

*

From his earliest childhood, Harold stood out in terms of his physical appearance. Particularly striking were his large, searching

---

21. Quoted in Goates, 26.
22. Quoted in Payne, "Louisa Emmeline Bingham Lee."
23. Gibbons, 15, 24.
24. Gibbons, 17.
25. Goates, 29.

brown eyes and abundant growth of dark, wavy hair. Harold's doting mother insisted on letting the young toddler's hair grow, and when it was sufficiently long, she fashioned it into ringlets in the style of Little Lord Fauntleroy. Louisa also made clothes for Harold worthy of his hair, white shirts with ruffles in front, starched cuffs, and a white middy draped over the shoulder of a handsome coat, all set off with a large black tie.[26]

Needless to say, Harold's dandy attire attracted unwanted attention at school. He became the butt of his classmates' jokes as they pulled his ringlets and taunted him for looking like a girl. All of this infuriated the young lad who found himself in more than a few fistfights and wrestling matches. Determined to end all such ridicule, Harold took his mother's scissors and cut off the front ringlets, which compelled his mother to shape his hair into a style more akin to that of his classmates.[27]

Harold was just five years old upon entering Clifton District School—some two years younger than his peers. He was allowed early entry because of his intelligence, combined with the fact that his mother had taught him the basics at home. Harold commenced his education at the same time his older brother, Samuel Perry, did. The two brothers developed a close relationship that continued throughout the course of their lives.[28]

Clifton District School, a rural institution, scheduled its classes around the demands of planting and harvesting, thereby accommodating the labor needs of the farms that formed the basis of the community's economy. During those times, Harold, along with his three brothers, assisted their father with the chores necessary to maintain their 100-acre farm. Its main crops included alfalfa, potatoes, and sugar beets. The family also had a small herd of dairy cows, chickens, and horses. "Our milk supply, as well as meat, eggs, and potatoes, and other vegetables were produced on the farm," recalled oldest son Samuel.[29] In general, "it was necessary for us to work hard

---

26. Gibbons, 18–19.
27. Gibbons, 19.
28. Gibbons, 20.
29. Recalled by Samuel Perry Lee, in Goates, 37.

7

on the farm and quite often there was little income to show for it," remembered Harold.[30]

The income generated by the small farm "made a bare living for the family." Thus, the elder Lee was compelled to seek additional outside income. "He held many different jobs to care for his family," Samuel recalled, including contracting with a company doing "custom drilling for artesian wells." Eventually, he managed to secured ownership of "the first siphon to carry water" into the region.[31]

Meanwhile, Harold moved ahead with his education at Clifton District School, developing a well-earned reputation as an outstanding student by the time he completed eighth grade. He also demonstrated talent as a musician, initially on the piano. He learned to play under the tutelage of a stern Scottish lady, Mrs. Sarah Gerard, who motivated her young pupil by rapping his knuckles at the sound of a sour note. He quickly became proficient to the point that he played for religious services at the Clifton Ward. Harold also mastered several wind instruments, specifically the baritone and French horns.[32] Harold likewise excelled at competitive sports, evolving into a well-coordinated athlete. Basketball was a favorite, as was fishing in the nearby mountain streams.

As he grew older, Harold's commitment to his LDS faith increased. As he later recalled: "Throughout my childhood there seemed to be a guiding hand over me."[33] Upon reaching his eighth birthday, Mormonism's "age of accountability" when one becomes responsible for one's own transgressions, he was formally baptized a member of the Church of Jesus Christ of Latter-day Saints, the ceremony performed outdoors in Bybee Pond.[34] Two years later, he was ordained a deacon in the Aaronic Priesthood. He was just ten. His early ordination resulted from the fact that his male classmates—all two years order—were being ordained, and ward leaders presumably did not want Harold to feel left out.[35]

---

30. Recalled by Harold B. Lee, in Goates, 37.

31. Rita C. Lee, "Life History of Samuel Perry Lee," June 1962, at https://www.family-search.org/photos/artifacts/10594539.

32. Goates, 46.

33. Quoted in Goates, 38.

34. Gibbons, 22–24.

35. Goates, 45.

One other religious experience had an important influence on young Harold. This involved a trip to Salt Lake City that Harold took with his father and older brother, Samuel. The elder Lee wanted his sons to see the home where he had been raised by his McMurrin grandparents and also to experience a session of the semi-annual LDS general conference. As Harold recalled: "I was just a young lad … sitting in the south gallery of the Salt Lake Tabernacle and looking down at the pulpit and seeing President Joseph F. Smith sitting there. I was impressed at seeing for the first time the President of the Church."[36] Harold also observed four members of the Council of the Twelve—all future church presidents—with whom he would one day closely work, namely, Heber J. Grant, George Albert Smith, David O. McKay, and Joseph Fielding Smith.[37]

*

After completing his first eight years of schooling at Clifton, Harold moved on to Oneida Stake Academy located in the county seat of Preston. The academy was owned and operated by the LDS Church as part of a network of LDS-sponsored schools throughout the Intermountain West. Oneida Academy accommodated both male and female high school students in two modern, recently constructed classroom buildings and a well-equipped gymnasium.[38]

Given the academy's relatively distant location—some eleven miles from Clifton—young Harold was compelled to live away from home. At just thirteen years old he was still wearing knee pants—underscoring the fact that he was the youngest student in the entire school. Thus, again, he stood out from his classmates. Harold's transition to his new environment was made easier given that older brother Samuel was also a student. The two brothers roomed together in a large boarding house near the academy.[39]

Harold quickly adjusted to his new environment. The standard courses included science, mathematics, biology, business, history, and

---

36. Quoted in Goates, 34.

37. Gibbons, 27. Joseph F. Smith died in 1918; his son Joseph Fielding Smith was ordained an apostle in 1910. So Harold's attendance at general conference probably occurred in the mid-1910s.

38. For a discussion of Oneida Stake Academy, see Fred E. Woods, "The Forgotten Voice of Oneida Stake," *Mormon Historical Studies* 4, no. 1 (Spring 2003): 81–100.

39. Goates, 46–47.

physical education, along with courses in LDS doctrine and missionary service.[40]

The teenage scholar was particularly drawn to the school's offerings in music, enabling him to further develop his talents on three different wind instruments—the alto horn, the French horn, and the baritone horn. He became so proficient on the baritone horn that he was invited to join the Preston Military Band—a community ensemble that performed at civic and patriotic events.[41]

Harold took an active interest in school sports. "My favorite sport was basketball," he recalled, "at the time … it was the major athletic sport" at the academy. "I gained considerable skill as a player," he continued, adding, "I was a member of the senior team that won the class championship."[42] Soon he was elected by his classmates as Student Manager of Athletics. In that position, he accompanied the school's athletic teams on the trips to play away games against rival schools. His responsibilities included handling business affairs and travel arrangements, as well as "scouting" rival teams at various locales as far north as Rexburg, Idaho, and as far south as Ogden, Utah.[43]

Upon reaching his senior year, Harold involved himself in yet another school activity—debate. Oneida Academy, along with other secondary schools in the region, engaged in a yearly round-robin debate competition. The two teams that made it to the final bracket were Oneida Academy and Fielding Academy, based in Paris, Idaho. The topic debated by Harold and his partner, Sparrel Huff, was "Whether or Not the Monroe Doctrine Should Be Abolished." The outcome proved a surprise win for Oneida. "We succeeded in turning the tables in a thrilling … decision over the Paris team," Harold remembered, adding, "we returned to Preston as conquering 'heroes.'"[44]

By the time of Harold's graduation from Oneida Stake Academy in the spring of 1916, he bore little resemblance to the thirteen-year-old boy in knee pants who had arrived three years earlier. Harold, or "Hal," as he preferred to be called by friends, had matured into self-confident young adult who left his mark on the school not just

---

40. Gibbons, 31.
41. Gibbons, 31.
42. Goates, 47–48.
43. Gibbons, 31.
44. Quoted in Goates, 47.

in classroom studies but also in a myriad of extracurricular activities. He had clearly inherited the drive and determination of his mother, excelling in virtually any enterprise he undertook.[45]

Harold's small graduating class consisted of just five girls and twenty-five boys—the latter whom he effusively characterized as "a great bunch of fellows."[46] He developed particularly close relationships with two classmates. One was his first serious girlfriend, Ethel Cole, from Fairview, Idaho. Harold described her as "my first 'sweetheart' and the only girl with whom I kept steady company with" during high school and for several years thereafter. In fact, up until 1920, "she and I kept up a rather, constant, intimate friendship either by correspondence or by occasional visits."[47]

The second classmate with whom he developed a more permanent relationship was Ezra Taft Benson. Benson, like Lee, was a native of Franklin County, born and raised in the tiny, unincorporated farming hamlet of Whitney—just south of Preston. Benson was an exact contemporary of Lee, having also been born in 1899, although Benson entered Oneida Academy in 1914, one year after Lee.[48]

During their academy years together, Lee and Benson became acquainted through their common interest in music. Both sang together in the school chorus and also performed with the academy band. Ezra played the trombone, Harold the alto trombone. Like Harold, Ezra was a passionate, proficient basketball player and member of the academy basketball squad.[49] Unclear, however, is the extent of their relationship, although Benson's biographer Sheri Dew asserts the two "became good friends."[50]

---

45. Gibbons, 33.

46. Quoted in Goates, 48.

47. Quoted in Goates, 47.

48. For four different book-length treatments of Ezra Taft Benson, see Francis M. Gibbons, *Ezra Taft Benson: Statesman, Patriot, Prophet of God* (Salt Lake City: Deseret Book Co., 1996); Sheri Dew, *Ezra Taft Benson: A Biography* (Salt Lake City: Deseret Book Co., 1987); and Mathew L. Harris, ed., *Thunder from the Right: Ezra Taft Benson in Mormonism and Politics* (Urbana: University of Illinois Press, 2019); and also Harris, *Watchman on the Tower: Ezra Taft Benson and the Making of the Mormon Right* (Salt Lake City: University of Utah Press, 2020).

49. Gibbons, 37.

50. Dew, *Ezra Taft Benson*, 38, states that the two men "became good friends" but offers no documentation. She may assume that their years spent as colleagues in the Quorum of Twelve Apostles cemented a preexisting friendship.

*

Immediately following graduation, Harold chose to pursue a career in education, prompted by the precarious financial situation of his family. Adequate family revenue proved a "major challenge" as his younger siblings came of age and their financial needs increased. Harold concluded that teaching could help him earn a sufficient income both to support himself and help his family. But in order to teach, he needed a teaching certificate from an accredited institution of higher learning.[51]

Harold chose Albion State Normal School located in the community of Albion, some 200 miles west of Clifton. To gain admission, he was required to pass an entrance examination testing his knowledge in fifteen different subjects. As Lee recalled, "I spent a very strenuous summer in intensive study, losing twenty pounds in weight, but I gained my objective, passing the required examination with an average grade of 89 percent."[52]

Thus, in June 1916, Harold departed Clifton for Albion where he enrolled for summer school classes at the normal (or teacher preparatory) school. Everything in the small town of Albion revolved around the school. "It was a quaint little old-fashioned town," Lee remembered. "Practically nothing was there but the school, which was splendid." Indeed, the complete absence of "all attractions that might detract from school"[53] kept him focused on his studies.

The young scholar found Albion State Normal School to be much different from Oneida Stake Academy in several respects. It was a larger institution, accommodating 300–400 students on a relatively large campus consisting of five red brick buildings on a grassy knoll. A state-funded school, its student body was drawn from all parts of the state. A significant number of its students and faculty were non-Mormon. The school's secular orientation was further reflected in a curriculum completely devoid of religion classes. Offered, instead, were classes like educational psychology and political science—topics new to the fledgling scholar. The entire academic environment represented Harold's first exposure to the outside world

51. Gibbons, 34.
52. Quoted in Goates, 48.
53. Quoted in Goates, 48.

beyond the Mormon-dominated upper Cache Valley. Lee found the new environment both stimulating and exciting.[54] He dubbed Albion Normal "a fine school, providing me some of the finest teachers of my lifetime."[55]

This being said, Harold held fast to his religious faith as a committed, practicing Latter-day Saint. He boarded with a local LDS family, the Burgesses, and also participated in the activities of the local LDS Albion Ward. Bishop Thomas Loveland recruited the musically talented Lee to be ward pianist.[56]

Harold attended Albion State over the course of two summers. During his first summer, he focused on his studies to the exclusion of extracurricular activities, enabling him to fulfill the requirements for preliminary teaching certification.[57]

Upon returning to Albion the following summer (1917), Harold completed a series of additional courses for advanced teacher certification, thus expanding his options as an educator. During that second summer, he also found time to exercise his musical talents as a member of the Albion Town Band and play on the Albion baseball team.[58]

Completing both summer sessions enabled Harold to move ahead with a career in education. Despite still being a teenager, he was anxious to do what he could to help his financially strapped family and looked forward to forging his own place as a productive member of society.

---

54. Gibbons, 36–37.
55. Quoted in Goates, 48.
56. Gibbons, 27.
57. Gibbons, 27.
58. Gibbons, 27.

CHAPTER TWO

TEACHER, MISSIONARY, AND MOVING TO SALT LAKE CITY

1916-23

The seven years from 1916 to 1923 represented a critical time for Harold B. Lee as he matured into manhood. Three developments facilitated his personal growth. The first was his four-year tenure as a teacher and then as a principal at two rural Idaho schools. The second was his two years of service as a full-time volunteer LDS missionary, including the challenges associated with that calling. And finally, after returning from his mission in 1922, came a change of residence for himself and the rest of the Lee family. All left Clifton, moving to Salt Lake City where they sought to adjust to its urban, more cosmopolitan environment.

*

Lee's first teaching assignment during the 1916–17 school year took him back to the upper Cache Valley and the rural Silver Star School, situated some five miles south of Weston, Idaho. The town of Weston itself, located on the Bear River, boasted a population of 450 residents.[1] Given Weston's distance from Clifton, eleven miles to the south, Lee obtained room and board with a local family. His teaching assignment paid $60 a month plus $15 for room and board.[2]

---

1. Among Weston's most famous residents was Parley Parker Christensen (1869–1954), a colorful political figure whose career ran the spectrum from the Republican Party to the ultra-radical Farmer-Labor Party, including an unsuccessful run for the US presidency in 1920. He was subsequently elected to the Los Angeles City Council, on which he served a total of six terms. For an overview of Christensen, see Newell G. Bringhurst and Craig L. Foster, *The Mormon Quest for the Presidency: From Joseph Smith to Mitt Romney*, 2nd ed. (Independence, MO: John Whitmer Books, 2011), 123–32.

2. Gibbons, 38–40.

The rookie educator found teaching in the one-room Silver Star School with its twenty-five rambunctious students extremely challenging. Lee provided instruction for grades one through eight, which necessitated extensive preparation. Never before had he confronted such a daunting task. As he later recalled: "I never worried so much over a work," but at the same time, "I learned some of the most valuable lessons of self-mastery of my life." As he further reported, the entire experience intensified his spirituality: "Almost nightly I placed my school problems before the Lord [and] the Lord never deserted me."[3]

Meanwhile, he stayed in close contact with his family, traversing the eleven miles between Weston and Clifton by horse to visit with his family on weekends. He turned most of his monthly salary over to his parents.[4]

The following academic year, 1917–18, Lee upgraded his teaching credential after completing his second summer of studies at Albion Normal School and used it to secure a better paying, less rigorous position. Lee's new position took him to Oxford, Idaho, located five and a half miles from Clifton. The two-story school building was the town's most impressive structure.[5] At Oxford District School, Lee's responsibilities involved not only teaching but also serving as school principal, supervising the school's two other teachers. These increased responsibilities netted him an increased salary of $90 a month.

Lee's teaching responsibilities proved less rigorous since the school's two other teachers, both women, taught the younger students. He provided instruction to and supervised students in grades seven through twelve. But this presented challenges of its own. Some students were, in fact, older and taller than their eighteen-year-old principal.[6]

The roughest of Lee's students attempted to drive him from his position. In response, the young principal challenged the ruffians on the basketball court. As Lee recalled, "My basketball experience stood in good stead. ... I dressed in basketball togs, and played with and against them, but as fortune would have it, I maintained

---

3. Quoted in Goates, 51.
4. Gibbons, 38–41.
5. Gibbons, 41. In today's dollars, Lee's monthly salary would equal about $2,000.
6. Gibbons, 42.

sufficient dignity to win their confidence as their principal, and also to win the kind of friendship that has lasted even to this day."[7]

The energic educator also organized the Oxford Athletic Club, made up of members of the larger community anxious to play competitive basketball. Playing forward on the first team, Harold and his team members traveled to neighboring towns where they engaged in spirited, aggressive competition—at times too much so. As Lee recalled, "Those were [the] days when the rules were lax, and I bear today scars of some of those encounters."[8]

During his time in Oxford, Lee confronted a more serious issue: the 1918 Spanish flu epidemic, which ravaged his community along with the rest of the state and nation. As he described it: "Our school was quarantined for some months. We had just reopened the school when every family [in the community] but two came down with the disease, and it became necessary for neighboring towns to assist in supplying food and nursing until their recovery."[9]

His duties as principal notwithstanding, Lee found time to pursue his love of music, which he freely shared with others. He provided piano and organ accompaniment at both school and community events. He also organized and trained the Oxford Ladies Chorus, which performed at a variety of local civic functions.[10]

Lee joined a dance orchestra organized by Dick and Chap Frew—two professional musicians who had recently moved to Oxford. The duo invited Harold to join their ensemble as a trombonist—a wind instrument he had never played but which he quickly mastered given his expertise on other wind instruments.[11] In addition to Harold, the five-member Frew Orchestra consisted of Dick Frew on violin, his brother Chap on the drums, Reese Davis on piano, and Marion Howell on cornet.

Lee's association with the Frew Orchestra took him on the road as the musical ensemble fulfilled a hectic schedule of engagements, performing at venues throughout southwest Idaho and northern Utah. As Harold recalled, "We were the only dance orchestra from

7. Recalled by Lee, in Goates, 53.
8. Recalled by Lee, in Goates, 53.
9. Recalled by Lee, in Goates, 53.
10. Gibbons, 42.
11. Gibbons, 43.

Logan, Utah on the south to Pocatello, Idaho on the north, and it was not usual for us to play two or three nights a week. ... On occasion it was almost morning before we arrived home. After a few hours rest I then went back to preside over the school."[12]

Such activity proved a mixed blessing for the young principal/musician. On the one hand, Harold's involvement with the Frew Orchestra was a significant source of additional income, thus enabling him to give to his father the entire amount of his school salary, significantly improving his family's fortunes. The income enabled his father to "modernize" the family home with running water and indoor plumbing. "We were about the first ones in the community to have a modernized home," recalled oldest son Perry, adding, "We felt like we were really living high." Samuel was able to buy "a secondhand Dodge" automobile at a time when cars were considered an "outstanding" item. Horses were still the standard mode of transportation in the small, relatively isolated agricultural community.[13]

At the same time, Lee's schedule took a toll on him physically. He contracted a serious case of pneumonia, ultimately recovering thanks to his mother who nursed him back to health.[14] Harold's tendency toward overwork worried both his mother and father.

Harold's parents manifested a second major concern connected with the Frew Orchestra. As recalled by Harold: "The Frews were always drinking when possible and indulging in conduct at a level far below what it should have been. I know that through those years, my folks 'held their breath' lest I allow this kind of association to overcome me."[15]

Harold's parents need not have worried; Harold continued active and faithful in his church callings. He served as elder's quorum president, presiding over men drawn from the Clifton, Oxford, and Dayton wards. He also served as organist of the Clifton Ward.[16]

*

Harold's commitment to his Mormon faith led to his service as

---

12. Recalled by Lee, in Goates, 55.

13. Recalled by Samuel Perry Lee, in Rita C. Lee, "Life History of Samuel Perry Lee." June 1962, at https://www.familysearch.org/photos/artifacts/10594539.

14. Gibbons, 44–45.

15. Recalled by Lee, in Goates, 55.

16. Gibbons, 45.

an LDS missionary—his call coming in September 1920, shortly after he turned twenty-one. He was assigned to serve in the Western States Mission, headquartered in Denver, Colorado. Prior to his departure, he obtained his endowments in the Logan Temple, accompanied by his father. His father's memorable parting words were: "Harold, my boy, your father and mother are looking for big things from you."[17]

The new missionary traveled on to Salt Lake City where he received a patriarchal blessing from presiding church patriarch Hyrum G. Smith. He was then formally set apart by Brigham H. Roberts, a member of the First Quorum of Seventy. Lee traveled next to Denver, arriving on November 11, 1920. He was greeted by mission president John M. Knight—who was destined to play a crucial role in Lee's development as a missionary and who would later serve as a mentor. The Western States Mission extended from North Dakota on the north to New Mexico on the south, and from western Colorado to eastern Nebraska.[18]

Lee was assigned to labor in Denver, among the largest cities west of the Mississippi River, boasting a population of some 250,000. The new missionary lamented, "No one was 'greener' and more unused to city life, than I was."[19] Denver was the fledgling missionary's "initiation into a new and alien world that bore little resemblance to the sheltered farming community where he was born and raised."[20]

Lee was initially assigned to labor with Willis J. Woodbury of Salt Lake City. Their main proselyting tools included door-to-door tracting and street meetings. The two missionaries' initial attempts at tracting proved less than successful, with the pair experiencing the humiliation of rejection, often accompanied by doors being slammed in their faces. Their first effort at conducting a street meeting also proved to be problematic.[21] As Lee recalled of his first encounter, "I thought I would surely faint, until I got started. I forgot myself and everyone else I'm afraid. ... I think if I keep on

---

17. Recalled by Lee, in Goates, 60.
18. Gibbons, 51.
19. Quoted by Lee, in Goates, 60.
20. As perceptively noted by Gibbons, 50.
21. Gibbons, 52.

finding out how little I know, by the time my mission is over I will be convinced I don't know anything."[22]

Such experiences prompted Lee and Woodbury to adopt what proved to be a more effective method of reaching out to potential converts. The pair drew on their combined talents as musicians—Lee as a pianist and Woodbury a cellist. In conducting their door-to-door tracting, the pair took Woodbury's cello with them. The instrument became an effective conversation piece. When householders learned that the duo were not selling cellos, but merely wanted to serenade them, the missionaries were invariably invited inside. If the home had a piano, the elders would make it a duet. The innovative method was successful.[23] As Lee described: "In every home we were complimented and invited back again. After playing and preaching we made real friends at each visit."[24]

Throughout the early months of his mission, Lee aggressively proselytized the message of Mormonism with unbounded energy and dedication. This caused him to muse, "If ever I felt like working, it is now when I am just beginning to appreciate the responsibility that rests upon me." He further added, "I am praying that I … can continue to do the work I am beginning to love."[25]

Lee's focused, hard-driven efforts impressed mission president Knight, who called on the energetic missionary to preside over the Denver Conference—the strongest and most productive region in the mission. In calling Lee to this position, Knight told him, "I am just giving you a chance to show what is in you." Lee's promotion came a mere nine months after his arrival in Denver.[26]

Upon becoming conference president, Lee made clear his determination to vigorously carry out his new responsibilities with maximum energy. "I am going to live up to the expectation made of me to the end that patience and strength will prevail," he said.[27] He further commented, "The crying responsibilities of today wake me

---

22. Quoted by Lee, in Goates, 60–61.
23. Gibbons, 52–53.
24. Quoted by Lee, in Goates, 61.
25. Quoted by Lee, in Goates, 62.
26. Gibbons, 54–56.
27. Quoted by Lee, in Gibbons, 58.

up to the fact that I must be working always if God is to accomplish anything through me."[28] Such remarks reveal his strong inner drive.[29]

As conference president, Lee oversaw the efforts of some thirty-five missionaries. He also presided over the various LDS branches (congregations) in Denver, Littleton, Boulder, Greeley, and Fort Collins. Lee assumed responsibility for performing marriages, conducting funeral services, and bestowing blessings and administering to the sick. Lee prepared and delivered sermons and even provided musical accompaniment when needed at church services.[30]

Lee imposed greater organizational efficiency and sought to improve missionary productivity. He pushed for an increased number of new converts while working to retain the loyalty of those who were already church members.

In pursuit of greater efficiency, Lee imposed a significant change on the duties of the conference president. Previously, the conference president was solely responsible for visiting and consulting with church members to address their needs and concerns—but that task required an inordinate amount of time and energy. Lee developed a more efficient system wherein the missionaries themselves took on the responsibility of "watching over the Saints"—a precursor to what later became the churchwide practice of "ministering."[31]

Further promoting missionary productivity, Lee encouraged "a healthy spirit of competition among the Elders."[32] This involved an increase in street meetings to two per week, along with intensified house-to-house tracting. Lee also increased the number of cottage meetings—supervised gatherings of members and non-members outside of regular church services. All of this produced a significant increase in convert baptisms. Lee reported seventy-two baptisms during the first nine months of 1922—more than had been reported the entire previous year.[33] In assessing the results, the hard-driving Lee stated that this is "the very condition I have wanted to see; and

---

28. Quoted in Goates, 63.
29. Gibbons, 58.
30. Goates, 63–64.
31. Goates, 64–65.
32. Quoted by Lee, in Goates, 58.
33. Gibbons, 57.

as a result, the pace is fast and furious and all will be well, if someone doesn't weaken."[34]

At the same time, Lee's intense leadership style, driven by high expectations, resulted on occasion in tension and outright dissent. "The jealousy and envy of some fellow workers brought much criticism with which he had to cope," noted Lee's son-in-law.[35] All of this caused Lee to muse, "Felt blue all day because of many griefs and complaints brought by the missionaries and from different Saints. Felt as inadequate as a babe and sure acted like one, too."[36]

Lee also expressed concern over the impact his missionary service had on his family's financial situation. In August 1922, his father informed him that while he "would never ask for [Harold's] release," he hoped that somehow God would "increase their [the family's] crops" so that Harold could stay. When he read his father's letter, Harold confessed, "I could cry when I think of it all, and my prayer is that God will make me humble so that I shall not disappoint them when I do go home."[37] In response to a letter from younger brother Clyde, Lee expressed a similar concern: "To think that I have caused my parents worry and hardship makes my heart ache. Sometimes I feel as though I couldn't stay to finish under the circumstances, but I've come to know out here that ofttimes when things are the blackest, just then things begin to happen. Never again, if I know it, will my folks be in the position they are in today."[38]

Finally, on December 14, 1922, came Lee's release from his mission. His missionary experience proved seminal for three reasons. Most important, the experience further facilitated the development of Lee's abilities as an organizer, leader, and achiever. Second, Lee developed a close relationship with mission president John M. Knight. As Lee himself stated, "I came to learn his virtues as well as his weaknesses. He was a fearless fighter in his missionary work and was always on the go, visiting the various divisions of the mission."[39] Indeed, Lee clearly embraced the latter two characteristics in his own actions and behavior.

---

34. Quoted by Lee, in Goates, 58.
35. Noted by Goates, 69.
36. Quoted from Lee's journal, in Goates, 66.
37. Quoted from Lee's correspondence, in Goates, 69.
38. Quoted from Lee, in Goates, 71.
39. Quoted from Lee's recollections, in Goates, 78.

Finally, Lee became acquainted with Fern Tanner—his future wife, who was likewise serving as a missionary. The two met in Denver immediately after Harold's arrival. The interaction was brief, as Fern was soon transferred to Pueblo, but the relationship was kept alive through periodic correspondence. After Fern's release in July 1922 and return home to Salt Lake City, the correspondence increased, with both anxious to continue their relationship on a personal level following Harold's release.[40]

His mission over, Lee traveled to Salt Lake City before returning to Clifton. Accompanying him was mission president Knight, who was returning to Salt Lake City in connection with his concurrent responsibilities as a member of the Ensign Stake presidency.

During Lee's stopover in Salt Lake City, Knight escorted his young protégé on a tour of the recently completed Church Administration Building at 47 South Temple Street adjacent to Temple Square. There Knight introduced Lee to a number of ranking church officials, including First Presidency counselor Charles W. Penrose and other notables, including Nephi L. Morris, John W. Wells, Richard R. Lyman, and Joseph Fielding Smith. Knight also invited Lee to a session of the Ensign Stake semi-annual conference. Much to Lee's surprise, Knight invited him to briefly speak to the congregation of over 1,000 worshippers in the Assembly Hall on Temple Square. In the congregation were a number of general authorities—the most notable, church president Heber J. Grant.[41] Lee also paid a courtesy call on Fern Tanner and took the opportunity to meet her parents—Stewart T. and Janet Tanner.[42] Finally, in late December, he returned home to Clifton and was reunited with his family.

*

Four months later, in April 1923, Harold decided to move from Clifton to take up residence in Salt Lake City. Lee's decision was motivated by three developments. Most fundamental, he concluded that his future was not in the upper Cache Valley, certainly not in farming, given the depressed conditions affecting agriculture during the period immediately following World War I. Clifton, along with

40. Gibbons, 75.
41. Goates, 23.
42. Gibbons, 74–75.

the entirety of upper Cache Valley, was particularly hard hit.[43] Even during the best of times, earning an adequate livelihood from farming proved difficult. Harold's own father was mired in debt, as were most other famers in the region. Clearly, farming did not appeal to Harold. Instead, he hoped to return to teaching—a field he found more fulfilling. However, Harold could not find a suitable teaching position in or near Franklin County.[44]

Further influencing Harold to depart was a major health problem—a severely painful hernia that required surgery. Given the limited medical facilities in Clifton, no doctors were available to perform the required procedure. Thus, Harold was compelled to travel to Salt Lake City where the operation took place in the LDS Hospital in February 1923, two months before he decided to leave Clifton permanently. During the extended period of recuperation that followed, Harold pursued his courtship of Fern Tanner. In fact, Lee convalesced in the Tanner home, where he became better acquainted with Fern's family. This, in turn, intensified the young couple's relationship, resulting in their decision to marry.[45]

The final factor triggering Harold's decision to leave his childhood home forever was his father's release as bishop of the Clifton Ward and subsequent disfellowshipment on April 1, 1923. Samuel Lee was found guilty of "Misappropriating Tithing Funds," not by a church court, which would normally be the case, but during a "Special Conference & Fast Meeting" conducted by Oneida Stake president Taylor Nelson. In attendance were two LDS general authorities: Apostle James A. Talmage and John Wells of the presiding bishopric. The order for this action came directly from the church's top leadership. President Heber J. Grant and members of the Quorum of the Twelve had deliberated on the matter on March 29.[46]

Samuel subsequently "made a public confession of his rong [sic]

---

43. As discussed in Thomas S. Johnson, *Agricultural Depression in the 1920s* (New York: Routledge, 1984). Also see James Grant, *The Forgotten Depression 1921—The Crash that Cured Itself* (New York: Simon and Schuster, 2014).

44. Gibbons, 77.

45. Gibbons, 80.

46. "Samuel Marion Lee Disfellowshipped," in Clifton Ward, Oneida Stake, Historical Record, 1922–26, Church History Library, Church of Jesus Christ of Latter–day Saints, Salt Lake City.

doing" at a May 5 sacrament meeting, asking "for the forgiveness of the people and also the blame to be laid on him and not his family." He further "stated that he was willing to make all rongs [sic] right even if it took his home to do so." He then pleaded for "the people to be kind to his family."[47]

Harold, still in Salt Lake City, expressed dismay upon first hearing of the action. Upon returning to Clifton, he penned the following: "Father and Mother have gone through a veritable hell and appear to have aged years since I last saw them. Even in the short time, I have been gone to Salt Lake, Father's hair is more gray than ever, and I am sure that only love and hard work will ever make back to them what they have lost."[48]

All of this reaffirmed Harold's decision to take up residence in Salt Lake City, a decision strongly endorsed by his family. As Harold wrote, "We [the family] have decided that I should work to get ahead, financially, so that I will return to Salt Lake and find employment as soon as possible. I am going to do the right thing, as the Lord directs."[49]

Soon thereafter, the rest of Samuel Lee's family moved to Salt Lake City. By March the Lee family was listed as residing in the Hawthorne Ward in the Granite Stake. The precipitating factor for the move was that "Samuel Lee sold their Clifton home to pay back the tithing money" he had misappropriated.[50]

*

By early 1923 twenty-four-year-old Harold Lee had proven his ability to survive beyond the limited confines of upper Cache Valley. His two years as a missionary in the metropolitan city of Denver helped to further instill the confidence needed to succeed in his new environment. Equally important, Salt Lake City was the headquarters of the LDS Church, which enabled the devout Latter-day Saint to gain a much better appreciation and understanding of all aspects of the faith that was becoming increasingly important in forming his identity.

---

47. "Samuel Marion Lee Disfellowshipped."
48. Quoted from Lee, in Goates, 83.
49. Quoted from Lee, in Goates, 83.
50. Noted in "Samuel Marion Lee Disfellowshipped."

CHAPTER THREE

MARRIAGE, CHURCH SERVICE, AND POLITICS

1923-35

For Harold B. Lee, the decade following his move to Salt Lake City altered his life in ways he probably could not have imagined. His marriage to Fern Tanner proved fortuitous in that she became an accommodating companion for the hard-driven, ambitious young man in a hurry. Lee's commitment to his LDS faith led to numerous church callings, each of increasing importance, culminating in his appointment as Pioneer Stake president. Lee was also drawn into the political arena when he was appointed to the Salt Lake City Commission in 1932.

*

Lee's most pressing concern upon arriving in Salt Lake City in April 1923 was securing gainful employment. He planned to resume his career in education but found that his Idaho teaching credentials were not valid in Utah. In order to secure a Utah credential, he was compelled to complete a series of required classes at the University of Utah during the summer. Subsequently, he found a position as a teacher/principal at Whittier Elementary School located in suburban South Salt Lake City.[1]

Lee then moved forward with his previously planned marriage to Fern Tanner. This took place in the Salt Lake Temple on November 14, 1923, with Apostle George F. Richards performing the ceremony. Lee was twenty-four; Tanner turned twenty-seven on their wedding day.[2]

---

1. Gibbons, 81–82.
2. Gibbons, 82.

Fern Lucinda Tanner was two and half years older than Harold and had a very different background and upbringing from her new husband's. Fern was the youngest of eight children born to Stewart Teft Tanner and Janet Coats. Stewart Tanner was the son of prominent Mormon pioneer Nathan Tanner. Stewart initially found success in mining and as a merchant. He also involved himself in local politics, initially serving on the board of the Salt Lake Canal Company and then on the Granger school board. Following that, he presided as a Salt Lake County justice of the peace.[3] Fern, along with her siblings, was raised in a comfortable urban environment, enjoying all the attendant privileges.

Fern was both well-educated and polished in demeanor. After completing high school, she attended LDS Business School. With her professional training, she secured a series of clerical positions, each of increasing status. She was initially employed by the Druchl Drug Company before moving on to the Salt Lake County Clerk's Office and finally to the office of Utah's Secretary of State. An active, practicing Latter-day Saint, Fern taught both in her ward's MIA and Sunday school programs. She, like Harold, developed a strong commitment to her faith. Fern also manifested talent as a musician, mastering both the piano and the organ. At the age of fourteen she was appointed organist of her ward's Primary.[4]

Fern, however, differed from Harold both in temperament and personality. Given her more urban background, she possessed a sophistication that Lee lacked. Thus, Fern instilled in her new husband much-needed qualities of refinement while introducing him to the art of "gracious, genteel living." Fern's sophisticating influence, in the words of a close family member, provided Harold "the balance and dimension ... to accomplish his destiny."[5]

Fern's temperament differed from that of her husband in a second way. When Harold dealt with a problem or issue, he was inclined to take "action promptly, regardless of whether [it involved] Church work, employment, or in a family setting." By contrast, Fern acted in

---

3. "S.L. Livestock, Mining Leader Dies in Granger," *Salt Lake Telegram*, Aug. 24, 1931.

4. Helen Lee Goates, "Fern Lucinda Tanner Lee: Her Life Story by Helen Lee Goates," courtesy of Craig L. Foster.

5. As recalled by Helen Lee Goates, in Goates, 137, 138.

a more restrained, deliberative manner, gently urging her husband to act similarly. "Now dear, you need to think about this, and you must not fail to look at the other side of the situation," she would carefully admonish him.[6]

Another of Fern's distinguishing characteristics was her quiet, unassuming, yet strong presence, which she used to influence important decisions. Most notable was her success in convincing her husband to change careers. As Harold recalled, "Fern was never content that I stay in the teaching profession,"[7] even though it provided "a safe and secure niche."[8] Specifically, Fern argued, teaching failed to provide income sufficient to meet the family's essential needs. Thus, Harold was compelled to seek supplemental income through additional employment both during the summer months and also part-time during the school year. Throughout his five years in education, he worked a variety of jobs. These included employment for Union Pacific as a watchman and train checker, for ZCMI as a grocery clerk, and for Bennett Gas and Oil. He tried his hand as a salesman initially with Swift and Company, and then for the Nash Automobile Company.

Finally, in the fall of 1928, at Fern's urging, Harold resigned his teaching position, leaving both education and the myriad of part-time jobs. Drawing on his sales experience, he accepted a position with Foundation Press. The new position involved sale of its publications—beautifully illustrated volumes containing stories drawn from the Bible. Foundation Press guaranteed Lee a salary of $50 a week plus commissions on "all sales of all the salesmen whom [he] trained." This change of profession represented a major turning point.[9]

*

Harold and Fern's lives changed yet again when they became parents, Fern giving birth to their first child, Maurine, on September 1, 1924. The birth proved difficult, and Fern suffered severe hemorrhaging that nearly took her life. Second daughter Helen followed fifteen months later on November 25, 1925. This birth proved

---

6. As recalled by Helen Lee Goates, in Goates, 137.

7. As quoted by Lee, in Goates, 86.

8. Gibbons, 159.

9. Goates, 85–86. Lee's 1928 annual salary was worth about $40,000 in today's dollars.

equally traumatic. Fern endured intense labor pains lasting for some sixty hours, leaving her weakened and debilitated.[10] From then on, Fern was never as healthy and strong as before, remaining in more or less "frail health" for the rest of her life.[11] As a consequence, the couple opted not to have any more children.

Harold reacted to his wife's health problems with compassion and sensitivity. He was continuously "solicitous of her and her needs, careful to make certain that she had all the modern, work-saving conveniences that would make life easier for her."[12]

As for his two daughters, Harold became a doting father, paying attention to their needs and concerns as often as his busy schedule would permit. Years later, he confessed, "I suppose it is the desire of every father to one day have a son. Daughters, yes, they are wonderful. But to have a son, I suppose, is the hope and desire of every father." Helen insisted, however, that if her father "were ever disappointed in not having a son, Maurine and I never knew that. He made us think that having two little girls were the greatest blessing he could have as a father."[13]

The Lees raised their daughters in a carefully structured environment, stressing obedience through positive reinforcement. Given that Maurine and Helen were separated in age by a mere fifteen months, they appeared as twins both in size and appearance. They were thus taught to do things together and to look out for each other.[14] Neither parent ever raised his or her voice when admonishing the girls, but approached tense, difficult situations in a calm, deliberative manner.[15]

Both daughters responded to their father's positive reinforcement. "Because we loved him so much, we tried hard to be what he thought we were, what he told us we were, so that we would not disappoint him. We didn't want him to find out that we really weren't as good as he thought we were. We always wanted him to be proud of us." At the ages of seven and eight, the daughters commenced their musical training, Maurine on the piano, Helen on violin—both seeking to

---

10. Goates, 84.
11. As remembered by daughter Helen Lee Goates, in Goates, 137.
12. Goates, 137.
13. As remembered by daughter Helen Lee Goates, in Goates, 120.
14. Gibbons, 160.
15. Goates, 135.

emulate their musically talented parents.[16] As Helen recalled, "They provided for us an atmosphere of love and peace," adding, "I realize that I had the ideal combination of parents: a father who was gentle beneath his firmness, and a mother who was firm beneath her gentleness. They worked as a team, equally yoked."[17]

*

Harold's position as a sales supervisor for Foundation Press allowed for an improvement in his family's standard of living, given his increase in salary. This permitted Harold to purchase a succession of larger, ever-nicer homes. From their first modest residence on 1538 West 800 South on Salt Lake City's west side, the family moved into a larger home next door at 1534 West 800 South. In 1928 the Lees moved a third time into an even nicer home less than half a mile away at 1310 Indiana Avenue—the residence formally owned by Fern's aging parents, who had moved into an assisted care facility. Eventually the Lees moved once more into a stately two-story home a mile and a half away at 1208 South 800 West, located on a large lot bordering the Jordan River.[18]

Moving up from the second-hand Model T Ford he purchased at the time of his marriage, Harold purchased a series of nicer automobiles over the years. He developed a preference for Buicks, recalls daughter Helen. Reliable transportation proved essential given Harold's constant travel for Foundation Press. His promotion to intermountain sales manager necessitated an even greater number of out-of-state trips. His wife and two daughters frequently accompanied him, turning such journeys into family vacations.[19]

*

Throughout this period, Harold Lee dedicated himself to a series of church callings, each of increasing importance and all at which he excelled. His first, upon joining the Poplar Grove Ward, was as M-Men instructor. It proved a challenging assignment given that the group of young eighteen-year-old-plus men "suffered from a lack of leadership."[20] Under Lee's guidance, the group of formally

---

16. Goates, 124.
17. Goates, 139.
18. Goates, 84–86, 125, 127.
19. Goates, 121.
20. As stated by Lee, in Goates, 87.

lethargic, indifferent young adults achieved success in a variety of competitive activities, earning for the ward a series of championships, specifically in basketball, debate, public speaking, and male quartet singing.[21]

Lee was next called as Poplar Grove Ward Sunday school superintendent. In fulfilling this position, he drew on his expertise in education, enabling him to significantly improve the quality of instruction. Next, he assumed the position of Pioneer Stake superintendent of education to oversee "a complete rejuvenation and reorganization" of the stake's educational system. Following that, Lee was called to the Pioneer Stake high council and ordained a high priest by Apostle Richard R. Lyman. Lee's meteoric rise continued when he was appointed in 1928 as second counselor in the Pioneer Stake presidency with President Datus E. Hammond and First Counselor Charles H. Hyde. Both men were significantly older than the twenty-nine-year-old Lee, each with long years of church service.[22]

*

Just two years later, in October 1930, Harold Lee was called to serve as Pioneer Stake president—the call coming directly from the LDS First Presidency and Quorum of Twelve Apostles. At thirty years old, Lee was the youngest stake president in the entire church. As his counselors, Lee chose Charles Sanford Hyde and Paul C. Child—the latter was Lee's former bishop in the Poplar Grove Ward.[23]

The Pioneer Stake, over which Lee presided, took its name from Pioneer Square where the first LDS settlers had camped upon their 1847 entry into the Great Salt Lake Valley. The stake of over ten thousand members consisted of ten wards and a branch of immigrants from Mexico. Situated southwest of downtown Salt Lake City, the stake was diverse in terms of the socio-economic status of its members. Its oldest section, containing the most substantial homes bordering the Jordan River, had been settled by early pioneer families. Among the most distinguished was the Cannon family, in particular, Sylvester Q. Cannon, son of George Q. Cannon. The younger Cannon had served as Pioneer Stake president prior to becoming presiding

---

21. Goates, 87; Gibbons, 83.
22. Gibbons, 88–89.
23. Gibbons, 89–92; Goates, 88.

bishop of the church in 1925. The eastern portion of the stake, which included much of the industrial section of the city, contained homes of simpler character. In between were neighborhoods of typical middle-class quality, akin to that in which the Lee family lived.[24]

Upon becoming stake president, Lee discovered a number of problems. While presiding over the reorganization of several of the ward bishoprics (a bishop and two counselors), he discovered acute shortages in one ward's tithing and building fund accounts, the result of a former bishop having deliberately misappropriated funds. Further complicating the situation, the accused former bishop was currently a member of the stake high council and a prominent popular member of the local community.[25]

Compelled by church protocol, the new stake president called and presided over a high council court—made up of Lee, his two counselors, and the other members of the high council—the very individuals with whom the accused high councilman currently served. This made for a stressful, awkward situation. As Lee recalled, "The trial involved the straining of relationships formed over a period of ten years." Thus, the high council court was deeply divided. Lee, along with counselors Hyde and Child, called for conviction, which involved the penalty of disfellowshipment. Members of the high council rejected the verdict—a surprising development. Lee promptly overruled the high council, declaring "that the decision of the [stake] presidency" would stand.[26] As Lee later recalled, "The suddenness of our decision ... seemed to stun" the high council, which ultimately affirmed the decision of the strong-willed stake president.[27]

Over the following months, Lee presided over a series of church courts in which offending stake members "were disciplined ... for a variety of transgressions, including adultery, fornication, polygamy, apostacy, and dishonesty."[28] As Lee recalled, among "the most trying were cases of those charged with immorality and adultery, one involving a nineteen-year-old girl, as well as one for alleged dishonesty

24. Gibbons, 89.
25. Gibbons, 92–93.
26. As recalled by Lee, in Goates, 89–90.
27. As recalled by Lee, in Goates, 90.
28. Gibbons, 94–95.

against a member of the high council."[29] Lee's revival of the previously dormant stake judicial system "had a bracing effect on the members of the stake, awakening them to the to the duties of membership" as practicing Latter-day Saints.[30]

*

In 1932, two years after becoming Pioneer Stake president, Lee confronted a much more serious problem among his parishioners—massive unemployment due to the Great Depression. Pioneer Stake was particularly hard hit in that some 50 percent of its working-age adults were unemployed—twice the national average. A survey of the 7,300 members of the stake revealed that more than half—4,800—needed help from outside the family to provide food, clothing, and shelter.[31]

Such widespread distress prompted Lee to develop a stake-based, self-help welfare program. Lee oversaw its implementation, working with his counselor Paul Child. Operation of the program involved negotiating contracts with local farmers to harvest their crops in exchange for a percentage of the bounty. The produce was then gathered to a central storehouse for distribution to needy members of the stake with the surplus canned for future use.

Operation of the storehouse was placed in the hands of unemployed Pioneer Stake members, thus giving them gainful employment. Other unemployed stake members were recruited to harvest the crops; still others were involved in processing the produce at the storehouse. Women mended and/or made clothing and bedding for destitute stake members.[32]

As the stake welfare program became fully operational, a system of entitlements was implemented. Those stake members who performed direct services, whether on the fieldwork crews or at the storehouse, were given "pay slips" which could be presented at the storehouse for food and/or other commodities. Those stake members who could not render service could secure permission from their ward bishops to obtain needed commodities.[33]

---

29. As recalled by Lee, in Goates, 90.
30. Gibbons, 95.
31. Gibbons, 110.
32. Gibbons, 110–11.
33. Gibbons, 111–12.

Also undertaken under the auspices of the Pioneer Stake relief program was the building of a stake gymnasium. Its construction, which commenced in 1933, provided employment for stake members who possessed skills as carpenters, masons, painters, bricklayers, and laborers. The cost of construction was funded in part through a $4,500 grant from the LDS First Presidency. Materials used in construction included rough lumber and bricks taken from nearby abandoned buildings. When completed, the Pioneer Stake gymnasium contained space for seven hundred parishioners, thereby providing "fully for [their] spiritual, physical, educational, and recreational needs."[34] Lee hosted church president Heber J. Grant and presiding bishop Sylvester Q. Cannon at a grand-opening celebration.[35]

Also in 1933 Lee had occasion to meet a second time with President Grant, albeit on a more serious matter. This meeting was prompted by questions concerning Lee's use of stake tithing funds to finance the stake welfare program. Lee and Child were both summoned to the Church Office Building where they met with Grant and his counselors, Anthony W. Ivins and J. Reuben Clark. Initially the First Presidency appeared both skeptical and negatively disposed, questioning such use of tithing funds. During the tense discussion, Lee sought to convince Grant that the funds had been properly authorized. Once convinced, Grant reportedly "banged his fist on the table to emphasize his support for the welfare program of the Pioneer Stake, saying 'Brethren, take care of your people, and that is the instruction from the First Presidency of the Church. If you need additional money, more than your tithing and fast offering, you are to come directly to the Presidency of the Church from now on and get the help you need.'"[36]

*

During this period, Lee changed careers, resigning Foundation Press to accept appointment to the Salt Lake City Commission—a full-time salaried position. Lee's unexpected entry into politics came in December 1932 when he was asked to fill the unexpired term of commissioner Joseph H. Lake, who had died earlier that year.

---

34. As quoted in Goates, 99.
35. Goates, 99.
36. As recalled by Paul C. Child, in Goates, 96–97.

The appointment of Lee came with the strong support of John M. Knight, himself a Salt Lake City commissioner. Knight was well-acquainted with Lee, having observed him as a successful, innovative missionary during Knight's tenure as Western States Mission president ten years earlier. Likewise supporting Lee was a second public official, Salt Lake City auditor Clarence Cowen, Lee's brother-in-law. Enhancing the appropriateness of Lee's appointment was Lee's residence in the city's westside—the region Joseph Lake had represented. In fact, Lee had lobbied on behalf of the city's westside for improvements in its transportation facilities.[37]

Lee, however, manifested some reluctance in entering the political arena, aware of its potentially unsavory aspects. As he confessed, "I entered my new work with considerable fear and many misgivings. Most of my close friends bemoaned my 'entrance into politics' as disastrous to my character and standing. Then too, I was entering the governing body of the city at a time when [its] finances and business affairs were precarious" given the ever-worsening effects of the Great Depression.[38]

By this time, however, Foundation Press was facing an uncertain future given a decline in the sales of its publications.[39] Ultimately, Lee's wife, Fern, gave her grudging approval, although, as with his close associates, she was less than enthusiastic about his entry into partisan politics.[40]

As a Salt Lake City commissioner, Lee joined John Knight and three other public officials in overseeing the city's municipal government. The most important of the these was Mayor Louis Marcus, elected a year earlier in November 1931. A native of Brooklyn, New York, and a non-Mormon, Marcus migrated to Utah in 1907. As a one-time businessman, he achieved success through Louis Marcus Enterprises, which owned a chain of theaters operating in Utah and Idaho. The other two city commissioners, George D. Keyser and Harry L. Finch, were likewise one-time businessmen and non-Mormons.[41]

---

37. Gibbons, 96–98; Goates, 106–108.
38. As quoted in Goates, 110.
39. Gibbons, 100.
40. Gibbons, 98.
41. Thomas G. Alexander and James B. Allen, in *Mormons and Gentiles: A History of Salt Lake City* (Boulder, Colorado: Pruett Publishing Co., 1984), provide an overview

The five-member Salt Lake City Commission assumed dual functions. Collectively, it exercised legislative authority over city affairs. Individually, each of the four commissioners, along with the mayor, oversaw the operation of a particular city department.[42]

Lee's assignment involved overseeing the Department of Streets and Public Improvements. The department was responsible for the repair and maintenance of all city streets, upkeep of its sewers and storm drains, and the collection of trash and garbage. Given the department's heavy workload, it utilized a labor force of 250 individuals—making it the second largest of the city departments. Lee oversaw a budget of a half-million dollars. However, the new commissioner was compelled to make significant cuts in staff given the continuing effects of the Great Depression.[43]

However, since Lee was completing the final year of his predecessor's term, he was immediately required to run for election to remain in office. The two-stage election process in November 1933 consisted of a primary election followed by a general election just two weeks later in which the final winner would be determined. In the primary, Lee faced a field of nineteen other candidates. Lee finished well out in front of his rivals with a total of 13,336 votes.[44]

Lee then moved on to the general election, running against the three contenders who had finished immediately behind him in the primary. Lee's prospects were complicated by the fact that in that same election, voters were considering a highly controversial ballot measure calling for repeal of the 18th Amendment—which had mandated prohibition. Lee opposed the measure. This prompted his three opponents to exploit the issue to Lee's disadvantage. Lee initially sought to avoid the issue, arguing that national prohibition was irrelevant in the city's municipal election. However, prohibition was thrust into the municipal campaign when the *Salt Lake Tribune*

---

of how Salt Lake City government evolved and operated during this period along with brief overviews of the various mayors and other public officials. See in particular, pp. 164, 147, 220, 172, 186, 205–207, 226.

42. Alexander and Allen, *Mormons and Gentiles*, 164.

43. Gibbons, 103–104; Goates, 111–13.

44. Gibbons, 106.

demanded in a strongly worded editorial that each of the four candidates publicly state his position on the issue.[45]

Under pressure, Lee stated that while he "was not satisfied with conditions as they were under Prohibition, I certainly could not sanction the old saloon conditions of the past." His opponents accused him of skirting the issue. As Lee recalled, "My opponents immediately attacked this statement saying I was dry, while others said I had 'straddled the fence,' but my good friends defended me and my position." He added, "Admittedly I was in an awkward position as a stake president running for office at a time when Salt Lake City was voting two to one to repeal prohibition."[46] In the end, Lee emerged victorious, garnering 29,336 total votes, with a comfortable 3,000-vote margin over his nearest challenger.[47]

At the same time, the ballot measure calling for the repeal of the 18th Amendment passed overwhelmingly, making Utah the thirty-fourth state to call for the repeal of prohibition nationwide through the approval of the 21st Amendment to the US Constitution.[48]

Over the following three years, from 1933 until 1936, Lee continued to discharge his duties over Streets and Maintenance. At the same time, he, along with his four fellow commission members, dealt with a number of significant issues. The most important, by far, was the city's effort to secure adequate federal funding for relief through the creation of jobs for individuals laid off as the Depression dragged on. The bulk of such funding came through an array of recently created New Deal agencies, including the Civil Works Administration (CWA), the Public Works Administration (PWA), the Federal Emergency Relief Administration (FERA), and the Works Progress Administration (WPA). Such programs, especially the WPA, had a long-lasting influence on Salt Lake City's economy and its landscape.[49]

Next to relief, the city's most difficult problem was maintaining an adequate supply of water. The demand for water by the city's 150,000 residents exceeded the supply, which was further aggravated

---

45. Gibbons, 107; Goates, 112.
46. As recalled by Lee, in Goates, 112.
47. Goates, 112.
48. Alexander and Allen, *Mormons and Gentiles,* 225.
49. Alexander and Allen, *Mormons and Gentiles,* 209–13.

by drought conditions. The city commission ultimately promoted three major projects to solve this problem: the development of additional deep-water wells; the Little Cottonwood project, which provided for the building of a seven-mile pipeline to bring water to the city from the nearby Little Cottonwood Canyon; and the Deer Creek project, providing for an aqueduct that would bring water to the city from Provo Canyon.[50]

A third problem confronting Salt Lake City commissioners was persistent crime and corruption. Prior to 1933 and the repeal of prohibition, much of the lawlessness stemmed from failed efforts to enforce the increasingly unpopular 18th Amendment. Such lawlessness continued into the mid to late 1930s, ultimately reaching into the ranks of the Salt Lake City Commission itself. Such corruption intensified following the departure of Mayor Louis Marcus in 1935. The competent Marcus lost his bid for reelection to Ernest B. Erwin—an automobile dealer who unexpectedly won on the unsubstantiated claim that Marcus was tainted by corruption. Erwin, over the course of his troubled tenure from 1935 to 1939 proved to be not only incompetent but corrupt in handling municipal affairs. In 1938 Erwin and Harry L. Finch—Salt Lake City police chief and former city commissioner—were accused of taking bribes from purveyors of prostitution and gambling. Following a series of lengthy trials, both were tried, convicted, and jailed.

Lee's response to Erwin and Finch is unclear. By this time, Lee had left the city commission to assume a full-time paid position as managing director of the LDS Church Welfare Plan.

---

50. Alexander and Allen, *Mormons and Gentiles,* 219–23.

CHAPTER FOUR

THE WELFARE PLAN
AND CALL TO THE APOSTLESHIP
1935-41

For Harold B. Lee, the six-year period from 1935 to 1941 proved momentous, given his increased prominence within both the LDS Church and the outside community. Thanks to his success with the Pioneer Stake welfare plan, the still-youngish stake president was enlisted to devise a similar program for the entire church. Appointed managing director of the Church Welfare Program in 1936, Lee devoted his time and energy to launching the program and overseeing its expansion over the following five years. This, in turn, led to his call to the apostleship, thereby joining the church's Quorum of the Twelve.

*

As early as 1932, church president Heber J. Grant called for "some special [churchwide] organization … to take care of those who are out of employment and in financial distress needing help."[1] Affirming Grant's proposal was J. Reuben Clark Jr. soon after his April 1933 installation as a counselor in the First Presidency. In a November 1933 statement, Clark outlined his rationale for a church-sponsored welfare program as an alternative to the New Deal relief programs which he denounced as "destroying our morale as a people and seriously undermining our morale and spiritual stamina" given their "greed, graft and corruption."[2]

Such calls from the church's top leaders notwithstanding, a churchwide program was delayed for four years as a consequence of

---

1. Heber J. Grant, as quoted in D. Michael Quinn, *Elder Statesman: A Biography of J. Reuben Clark* (Salt Lake City: Signature Books, 2002), 388.
2. J. Reuben Clark, as quoted in Quinn, *Elder Statesman,* 389.

disagreements among general authorities over the need and viability of such a program.[3] In the meantime, church leaders delegated responsibility for providing relief to local stake presidents, the most prominent being Harold B. Lee, whose Pioneer Stake program caught the attention of Grant and other church leaders.[4]

*

Finally, in April 1935, the thirty-six-year-old Lee was summoned to meet with Grant and his new second counselor, David O. McKay, to discuss a churchwide relief program. J. Reuben Clark, the proposed program's strongest proponent, was out of town.[5] The federal government's intention to shift the burden of relief to the states and local governments, combined with the fact that many LDS wards had fallen short in meeting the welfare needs of their members, prompted the church leaders to move forward.[6]

During the meeting, "President Grant said he wanted to take a 'leaf out of Pioneer Stake's book' in caring for the people of the Church."[7] Thus, he assigned Lee "to work out a program of relief for the entire Church."[8]

In recalling his meeting years later, Lee revealed his initial feelings of inadequacy. "There I was, just a young man in my thirties. My experience had been limited. … And now, to put me in a position where I was to reach out to the entire membership of the Church was one of the most staggering contemplations that I could imagine. How could I do it with my limited understanding?"[9] Upon leaving the meeting, he withdrew to a secluded spot where he "knelt in prayer and sought the guidance of an all-wise God in this mighty undertaking."[10] In the days that followed, he "sought the counsel of a number of prominent men," including Reed Smoot (an apostle and former US senator), John M. Knight (Lee's former colleague on the

---

3. Among those opposed were First Presidency counselor Anthony W. Ivins and presiding bishop Sylvester Cannon; Quinn, *Elder Statesman*, 390–92.

4. James B. Allen and Glen M. Leonard, *The Story of the Latter-day Saints*, 2nd ed. (Salt Lake City: Deseret Book Co., 1992), 521.

5. Goates, 141.

6. Allen and Leonard, *Story*, 521.

7. As recalled by Lee, in Goates, 141.

8. As recalled by Lee, in Goates, 142.

9. As recalled by Lee, in Goates, 142.

10. As recalled by Lee, in Goates, 142.

Salt Lake City Commission), and Paul C. Child (currently overseeing the Pioneer Stake welfare program).[11]

Over the following two months, Lee prepared a preliminary report outlining his proposals for a churchwide program, which he submitted to Grant in June 1935. Grant, in turn, called for a churchwide survey to determine relief needs within the church. Completed in September 1935, the survey found that 88,480 members, or 17.9 percent of the total church population, received some form of relief. The majority of those individuals—80,555, or 16.3 percent—received such aid from public sources—local, state, and/or federal government. Whereas a mere 1.6 percent, or 7,907, received assistance from the LDS Church. Equally revealing, the report stated that between 11,500 and 16,500 of church members on relief did not require such assistance.[12]

Using this information, Lee prepared a revised report, which he presented to the First Presidency in March 1936. One month later, the Church Security Program was officially launched—its name formally changed to the Church Welfare Program two years later. The program's purpose, as officially stated, was "to set up ... a system under which the curse of idleness would be done away with, the evils of a dole abolished, and independence, industry, thrift, and self-respect be once more established amongst our people. The aim of the church is to help people help themselves. Work is to be re-enthroned as the ruling principle of the lives of our church membership."[13]

*

Lee was appointed the new program's managing director and provided office space in the Church Administration Building. He immediately resigned as a Salt Lake City commissioner even though his term did not end until January 1938. He did, however, retain his calling as Pioneer Stake president.

As managing director, Lee was directly responsible to the Central Security Committee chaired by Apostle Melvin J. Ballard. Other members of this committee, which provided oversight, included

---

11. Goates, 142–43.

12. As reported in Leonard J. Arrington and Wayne K. Hinton, "Origin of the Welfare Plan of the Church of Jesus Christ of Latter-day Saints," *BYU Studies* 5, no. 2 (Winter 1964).

13. *Conference Report*, Oct. 1936, as quoted in Gibbons, 134.

Henry D. Moyle, Mark Austin, Campbell M. Brown, Stringham Stevens, and William E. Rayberg.[14]

In implementing the program, Lee oversaw the creation of thirteen regions consisting of all LDS stakes in Utah, Idaho, California, and Arizona. Lee appointed a stake president in each of the thirteen regions to serve as regional chairperson. The remaining stake presidents in each region served on an advisory council overseeing the program. Within each stake, local security councils were formed, composed of ward bishops, with one of their number designated as chairperson. At the grassroots level, the existing priesthood and auxiliary organizations within each ward provided the personnel to carry out the program locally.[15] In sum, "the vast machinery of the Church welfare plan reached into every corner of the Church"—according to Harold Lee himself.[16]

Lee personally supervised the training of the regional chairs and other key staff responsible for carrying out the program. This required him to spend a significant portion of his time out of town, traveling throughout the Intermountain West. Joining Lee on many of these trips was Apostle Melvin J. Ballard, whose presence affirmed the importance of the program. Heber J. Grant attended advisory committee meetings, thereby bestowing the imprimatur of the First Presidency.[17]

At the local level, ward bishops oversaw the activation of priesthood quorums and Relief Societies, which assumed responsibility for determining where the greatest need existed, discovering the most destitute families, and providing immediate relief—primary attention being given to emergency cases.[18]

Further acting at the ward level, Relief Society women sewed quilts and clothing and secured canned foods for distribution. Ward priesthood quorums leased land and obtained farm equipment to provide employment and produce food. Ward bishops helped

---

14. Gibbons, 129.
15. Gibbons, 130–31.
16. Harold B. Lee, "The Church Security Program in Action," *Improvement Era*, Dec. 1936, 740–41.
17. Gibbons, 131.
18. Allen and Leonard, *Story*, 523.

employable members to become self-sufficient through the creation of employment committees.[19]

The Church Welfare Committee established employment offices, separate from local wards, to further assist those seeking employment. Also established were programs providing vocational training for unskilled workers. Wards teamed up with local schools to develop training classes in bricklaying, carpentry, plumbing, and other trades.[20]

The mainstay of the welfare program was productive agriculture, wherein both idle land and unemployed people were put to work. Such activity stood in contrast to the New Deal Agricultural Adjustment Act, which mandated a reduction in agricultural production in order to raise farm prices. The church welfare program affirmed instead that an abundance of farm produce offered the best means of alleviating distress.[21]

*

The welfare program produced results, evident during its first year of operation. Some 15,000 Latter-day Saints transferred from government to church relief.[22] Moreover, the program, according to Lee, boasted twenty-eight categories of projects undertaken. These included canning or drying fruits, vegetables, and meats; sewing; farming; shoe manufacture and repair; logging; coal mining; manufacture of temple and other garments; and making cement building blocks, sorghum, molasses, furniture, toys, mattresses, and disinfectants.[23]

Over the four-year period from 1937 through 1941, Lee oversaw the addition of new facilities to carry out the program. In 1937, the Cooperative Security Corporation was established to handle the program's legal and financial transactions.[24] That same year, the first Bishop's Storehouse opened in Salt Lake City. This facility formed the basis of Welfare Square, which commenced operations in 1939 with a large storehouse and cannery. Over the

---

19. Allen and Leonard, *Story*, 523.
20. Allen and Leonard, *Story*, 524.
21. Allen and Leonard, *Story*, 524.
22. Allen and Leonard, *Story*, 525.
23. Lee, "Church Security Program in Action," 740–41; also noted in Gibbons, 136.
24. Gibbons, 140.

following two years a grain elevator was added along with a milk processing plant.[25]

*

The impact of the welfare program drew attention from outside the LDS community. In a 1937 article, *Reader's Digest* extolled its virtues: "A year ago 84,460 Mormons, about one-sixth of the entire Church, was on direct relief. Today none of them are. The Church is taking on its own. ... Within a year every one of the 84,460 Mormons was removed from the government relief rolls all over the country."[26] The program also earned the praise of US president Franklin D. Roosevelt, who expressed the hope that the program "might inspire other groups to do something of a similar nature."[27]

At the same time, the program drew criticism from certain officials within the church itself. Apostle Stephen L. Richards called upon the church "to leave the money side of relief to the Government" while confining "itself to spiritual and character rehabilitation."[28] Likewise opposed was presiding bishop Sylvester Q. Cannon, who had questioned the program from its beginnings.

In reaction, First Presidency counselor J. Reuben Clark—among the program's strongest backers—assailed Cannon. "For four years he [Cannon] has either fought the Plan the Presidency then proposed or has willfully failed to support it," Clark wrote, adding that Cannon should decide "to get in line or to get out of the way."[29] Ultimately, in April 1938, Cannon was released as presiding bishop. Shortly thereafter he was appointed to a vacancy in the Quorum of the Twelve.[30]

Clark played a major role in promoting the welfare program. Commencing in 1937, he attended meetings of the Central Security Committee on a regular basis. As a result, the sixty-six-year-old Clark and the energetic Lee developed a close working relationship, Clark assuming the role of mentor. Over time Clark came to

---

25. "Timeline: A Look Back at the Church Welfare Plan," *Church News and Events*, https://www.churchofjesuschrist.org/church/news/a-look-back-at-the-church-welfare-plan?lang=eng.

26. Marc A. Rose, "The Mormons March Off Relief," *Readers Digest*, June 1937, 43–44.

27. As quoted in Arrington and Hinton, "Origins of the Welfare Plan," 81.

28. As quoted by J. Reuben Clark, in Quinn, *Elder Statesman*, 400.

29. As quoted by J. Reuben Clark, in Quinn, *Elder Statesman*, 400.

30. Quinn, *Elder Statesman*, 401.

regard his protégé almost as a son. Lee, in turn, became increasingly dependent on the older, wiser Clark. On one memorable occasion, when Lee sought advice concerning the opposition he faced from some general authorities in implementing a particularly controversial policy, Clark simply stated, "Look, Kid, you continue to follow the course and it won't be long before they will all want to jump on the bandwagon."[31]

In assessing the Church Welfare Program's impact, several facts stand out. Most significantly, the program provided assistance to tens of thousands of Latter-day Saints. By 1939, as the program reached its Depression apex, it provided assistance to 155,460 Saints.[32] But at the same time, an array of New Deal programs "dwarfed the Church's sharing and self-help activities." During the 1930s, up to three-fourths of Utah's rural population received federal relief. The Works Progress Administration employed an average of eleven thousand Utahns annually, and the National Youth Administration enrolled an average of 2,200 Utahns per year. Moreover, a higher proportion of LDS Utahns obtained federal relief than did non-LDS Utahns.[33] Thus, while church relief helped, it could not provide all the assistance needed.

*

In 1941, looking back on his early years as managing director, Harold Lee simply remarked, "For five glorious, strenuous years I have labored under a call from the First Presidency, with a group of select brethren" to oversee the program's "development" and "unfolding." To those who inquired, "Well, Brother Lee, how is the new welfare program going in the Church?" Lee had a stock answer: The program is "just as good as the individual stake presidents want it to go."[34] Lee's frank, direct response reflected his unerring focus on the task at hand combined with a blunt, no-nonsense demeanor.

Such unpretentiousness aside, Lee's highly visible role in developing the Church Welfare Program caused observers both within and outside the LDS community to view the energetic administrator

---

31. As related to Frances Gibbons by Lee, in Gibbons, 139.
32. Quinn, *Elder Statesman,* 403.
33. Quinn, *Elder Statesman,* 403–404.
34. Lee, as quoted in Goates, 155.

as a potential candidate for political office. Throughout the early to mid 1940s, Lee was urged to return to the political arena. The first of these calls came in 1940 when political operatives called on him to run as a Republican for Utah governor. This prompted Lee to seek the advice of J. Reuben Clark. Worried that 1940 "was not a good year to run," Clark urged Lee "to wait."[35]

Four years later, in 1944, Lee was again urged to run for governor, this time approached by "a delegation of Republican legislators" along with a host of prominent state Republican leaders, including Salt Lake City commissioner George D. Keyser, Price City mayor J. Bracken Lee (no relation), and Arthur V. Watkins, chair of the Utah County Republican Party. Again, Lee consulted Clark, who reached out to fellow First Presidency counselor David O. McKay. Clark and McKay felt that Lee "should not run for office because of the need of [his] services" in the church.[36]

Two years later, in 1946, one last effort was made to lure Lee back into politics, on this occasion as a candidate for the US Senate. Utah Republican leaders vigorously lobbied him to run against incumbent Democratic senator Orrice Abram "Abe" Murdock Jr. These Republicans, moreover, had consulted with First Presidency counselors Clark and McKay, who initially seemed inclined to allow Lee to run, given that Senator Murdock appeared vulnerable in 1946—a year marked by Republican ascendancy. Despite this, Lee declined, having failed to secure permission from church president George Albert Smith, who was out of town at the time and unavailable for consultation. In the end, Murdock was defeated by Arthur V. Watkins—the Republican operative who had urged Lee run for political office some four years earlier. Thus ended Lee's direct involvement in partisan politics.[37]

*

Lee's future lay in service to the LDS Church, and his increasingly close working relationship and friendship with J. Reuben Clark proved crucial in this undertaking.

---

35. J. Reuben Clark, Office Diaries, Mar. 2, 1940, copies of originals located in BYU Special Collections Library, courtesy of Reid Moon.

36. Goates, 185.

37. Goates, 186.

That Lee and Clark were drawn toward one another is not surprising given the similarities in their backgrounds and personalities, even though the two were a generation apart in age. Clark, like Lee, came of age under humble circumstances. Born in 1871, Joshua Reuben Clark was the oldest of ten children, raised in the tiny Utah community of Grantsville (west of Salt Lake City) where his father struggled to support his large family as a schoolteacher. Young Reuben, again like Harold, demonstrated considerable intelligence from an early age along with a drive to excel. Clark initially became an educator after graduating from the University of Utah in 1898 first in his class.[38]

Clark's ultimate ambition was to be a lawyer, which he became upon receiving an L.L.B from Columbia University in 1906. From there Clark embarked on a career as a US diplomat, ultimately serving as an ambassador to Mexico and as US Under Secretary of State. Meanwhile, he established a law firm in Salt Lake City in partnership with Staynor Richards and Albert Bowen. His LDS Church service commenced in 1925 with his appointment to the general board of the Young Men's Mutual Improvement Association (YMMIA). Clark's 1933 appointment to join the First Presidency as second counselor came as a surprise since he had never served in a leadership position at either the ward or stake level. In fact, he was ordained an apostle to serve in the presidency but, at this initial stage, did not join the Quorum of the Twelve. Church president Heber J. Grant insisted on his appointment, aware of Clark's intelligence, political connections, and talents as a proven administrator. This latter quality was akin to that possessed by Clark's protégé Harold Lee. Both Clark and Lee, moreover, promoted conservative views of church doctrine and practice.[39]

In the wake of his appointment, Clark played an increasingly important role in overseeing church affairs during the 1930s. He emerged as de facto church leader in 1940 after Grant suffered a stroke that left him a semi-invalid up until the time of his death in 1945.[40]

*

---

38. The definitive work on the life and career of Clark is Quinn, *Elder Statesman*.
39. Quinn, *Elder Statesman*, 14–48.
40. Quinn, *Elder Statesman*, 91–106.

In 1941 Clark pushed for the elevation of Lee to the apostleship following the death of Apostle Reed Smoot.

Smoot, both prominent and controversial, had been a member of the Twelve for over forty years, first appointed to that body in 1900 and concurrently serving as a US senator. His election in 1903 drew national attention to the Latter-day Saints and their recently abandoned practice of plural marriage when senators questioned Smoot's fitness.[41] After four years of deliberations, Smoot was seated. Thirty years later, Smoot generated further national notice through his co-sponsorship of the controversial 1932 Smoot–Hawley Tariff. Thus, the appointment of Harold Lee—barely forty-two years old—to replace Smoot attracted widespread attention.[42]

Lee himself vividly remembered the events leading to the lifetime calling. His initial awareness occurred in late March 1941 following a stake conference at which he was the featured speaker. Also in attendance were J. Reuben Clark and his wife, Luacine. In a casual conversation afterwards, Clark hinted at Lee's possible appointment. Luacine was even more direct in disclosing "my appointment as the new Apostle." Lee further mused, "I thought he [Clark] was only joking, but I learned that this was his way of preparing me for the shock that was coming to me at the April Conference."[43]

The actual call came on April 4 during the course of that conference when Lee was summoned to a private meeting with President Grant who was able to announce "to me that I had been named to be elevated to the Quorum of the Twelve." Lee's initial response to the eighty-four-year-old leader was, "Do you really think I am worthy of such an exalted calling?" According to Lee, Grant simply replied, "If I didn't think so, my boy, you wouldn't be called."[44]

Lee was formally sustained the following day by the church faithful in attendance. Upon taking his place on the stand among his fellow apostles, Lee clearly stood out for his youth. The next junior

---

41. The standard work on this event is Kathleen Flake, *The Politics of American Religious Identity: The Seating of Reed Smoot, Mormon Apostle* (Chapel Hill: University of North Carolina Press, 2003).

42. For an overview of Smoot's life, see Milton R. Merrill, *Reed Smoot: Apostle in Politics* (Logan: Utah State University Press, 1990).

43. As recalled by Lee, in Goates, 156.

44. As recalled by Lee, in Goates, 157–58.

apostle, Sylvester Q. Cannon, was twenty-two years Lee's senior and had snowy white hair. Lee's daughter Helen recalled the scene: "There stood Brother Cannon, tall and stately with his beautiful white hair, and next to him was my father, who was much shorter, with his black hair, which gave him a youthful appearance." With characteristic Lee family frankness, she added, "He almost looked like he didn't belong, for he was much younger than the youngest of the men."[45] Lee, aware of his status as the most junior of the apostles, mused, "I came to know what it meant to be at the 'foot of the ladder.'"[46]

*

In fact, Lee's status as the Twelve's most junior member at the "foot of the ladder" would prove short lived. He would soon find himself standing at the vanguard of a new generation of church leaders called to the Twelve over the following four years. Two of these, Spencer W. Kimball and Ezra Taft Benson, were also in their forties when called in 1943, and, like Lee, would eventually ascend to the presidency. In 1944, Mark E. Petersen, also in his forties, joined the quorum, as did forty-eight-year-old Matthew Cowley a year later.[47]

Throughout the 1940s, Harold Lee, working closely with this quartet of young, energetic apostles, would exert increasing influence on both church policy and its organizational structure, doing so under the guidance of his mentor, J. Reuben Clark.

---

45. As recalled by Helen Lee, in Goates, 162.
46. As recalled by Lee, in Goates, 162.
47. Goates, 162.

CHAPTER FIVE

FROM JUNIOR TO SENIOR APOSTLE
1941-51

For Harold B. Lee, the ten-year period from 1941 to 1951 proved crucial as the newest apostle found himself confronting a myriad of duties and responsibilities. Lee, exercising both dedication and hard work, quickly emerged as a major figure within the Quorum of the Twelve. He earned the respect of his peers as he proved that he could be counted on to tackle and find solutions to whatever problems the quorum dealt with. The decade itself was marked by a series of traumatic events: World War II, post-war adjustments, and the Korean Conflict. Each presented unforeseen challenges for the LDS Church.

*

Lee continued in his post as managing director of the Church Welfare Program, which consumed a major portion of his time and energies. Easing this burden somewhat was Marion G. Romney, the new assistant managing director and newly ordained assistant to the Twelve. Romney was born in Mexico, raised in Idaho, and educated in Utah, where he practiced as a lawyer prior to being called to church service.[1]

At the same time, Lee was assigned other responsibilities, among the most important was a hectic schedule of conducting stake conferences. This duty necessitated frequent out-of-town travel on weekends to communities not just within Utah and adjoining western states, but on occasion to distant parts of the United States, including the West and East Coasts, the Midwest, and the Southeast. A second major duty involved performing marriages, most often in the Salt Lake Temple.[2]

---

1. For an overview of Marion G. Romney's career, see Howard F. Burton, *Marion G. Romney: His Life and Faith* (Salt Lake City: Bookcraft, 1988).
2. Gibbons, 165–72.

Lee was also a featured speaker at various church-sponsored events. This latter assignment caused him feelings of inadequacy, making him "conscious of [his] limitations" and wishing he could speak with "more freedom." Over time he gained greater confidence. Nevertheless, he continued to approach each speaking assignment "with a certain trepidation."[3]

As managing director of church welfare, Lee was sometimes called to deal with emergency situations involving church members. In October 1941, he traveled to the Gila Valley in southwestern Arizona in response to a disastrous flood that swept through the region. The Gila River overran its banks, converting farmland into a lake. Total losses in land and property for church members in the region amounted to some $100,000 (in excess of $1.7 million today). There to meet Lee was Spencer W. Kimball—the forty-six-year-old president of the local Mount Graham Stake. Along with Marion G. Romney, who accompanied Lee, the three church officials toured the region to assess the damage.[4]

This catastrophic event was noteworthy for three reasons. First, it represented the first major test of the Church Welfare Program in a disaster situation. Lee brought to the fore his skills in marshaling "the energies and talents of numerous people to" oversee the distribution of needed aid. Second, Kimball demonstrated his own talents in lifting the "morale of the people" while setting them to work, fighting the flood, and repairing the damage once the waters had subsided. In fact, Lee was so impressed with Kimball's leadership that upon his return to Salt Lake City, he alerted J. Reuben Clark of Kimball's fitness for a position of greater leadership—which occurred two years later when Kimball was called to join the Twelve.[5]

Throughout this period, Lee, as church welfare director, worked closely with Salt Lake City attorney Henry D. Moyle, who chaired the General Welfare Committee. The two men's relationship was "not always placid." Both "were strong-minded with opinions they did not yield easily. Both were self-confident."[6] Moyle was the older

---

3. As quoted in Gibbons, 172.

4. For a discussion of Spencer W. Kimball's role in this event, see Edward L. Kimball and Andrew E. Kimball Jr., *Spencer W. Kimball* (Salt Lake City: Bookcraft, 1977), 176–79.

5. Gibbons, 172–73.

6. This is according to Gibbons, 176.

by some ten years. Lee, however, enjoyed apostolic seniority, having been ordained to the Twelve in 1941, whereas Moyle was not called to the apostleship until 1947.

Moyle and Lee came from different socio-economic backgrounds. Lee struggled financially during his early years; Moyle, the son of a successful Salt Lake attorney, businessman, and politician, was raised in affluence and privilege. Moyle, moreover, was educated at major universities in Europe and the United States, and subsequently established himself as a prominent attorney and businessman.[7]

The two men harbored "vastly different ... perceptions about the poor and the needy," which was reflected in their views on how best to carry forth the welfare program. Lee promoted caution and restraint in handling its finances, and "follow[ed] policy guidelines with exactness." Moyle was less cautious in adhering to financial guidelines and was willing to cut through red tape to achieve results. These differences sometimes brought the two into direct conflict, creating instances where "they outspokenly opposed each other."[8] The strong-willed pair periodically clashed over issues involving church finances during the subsequent two decades.

*

Lee faced a different set of challenges as war clouds gathered in Europe and Asia during the late 1930s and into the early 1940s, culminating in America's entry into World War II in December 1941.

Some two years earlier, church leaders urged American neutrality in response to Nazi Germany's invasion of Poland and the formal commencement of World War II in September 1939. J. Reuben Clark was particularly outspoken, declaring, "We would not settle it by joining the conflict," and adding, "this is one of those questions which can be settled only by the parties themselves by themselves." The sole role for the United States, he concluded, was that of "peacemaker."[9]

As war intensified, church officials ordered the withdrawal of all proselytizing missionaries from Europe, Asia, and the Pacific, leaving church members in those regions on their own. Most adversely

---

7. Gibbons, 176–77.
8. Gibbons, 177.
9. J. Reuben Clark, "In Time of War," *Improvement Era* 42 (November 1939): 657, as quoted in Allen and Leonard, *The Story of the Latter-day Saints*, 2nd ed. (Salt Lake City: Deseret Book Co., 1992), 538.

affected were some 15,000 church members living in Nazi Germany—the largest number of Latter-day Saints living outside the United States. Missionary activity in other regions, including North and South America, was drastically curtailed.[10]

Lee was quickly caught up in the debate over America's role in the ongoing hostilities. In late November 1941, while on a train trip to Oakland, California to fulfill a stake conference assignment, he found himself in a discussion with two government officials involved in defense work. Of his conversation, Lee noted: "I found them wholly in support of the idea that nothing short of complete [American] participation would suffice the present situation."[11]

Indeed, just days later, on December 7, 1941, the Japanese launched a surprise attack on Pearl Harbor. As Lee noted: "Received word over the radio that Japan had attacked at Hawaii and Philippines with heavy losses."[12] In the attack, 2,335 military personnel were killed, including a number of Latter-day Saints. Among these was Captain Mervyn Sharp Bennion, who hailed from a prominent LDS family and was the son-in-law of J. Reuben Clark. Bennion was in charge of the battleship *USS West Virginia* on the day of the attack and refused to leave his post. For his bravery, Bennion was posthumously awarded the Congressional Medal of Honor. Clark, who harbored deep pacifist views, was shaken by the news.[13] He "showed deep emotion as he spoke of the death of the son-in-law" whom he loved as a son.[14]

In the wake of Pearl Harbor, Americans became jittery to the point of paranoia, including residents in the LDS-dominated Great Basin. In Salt Lake City, streetlights were turned off at night and windows were shrouded. Members of the Veterans of Foreign Wars were assigned to guard the facilities at Welfare Square against possible Japanese attack. Some church members went so far as to hoard food in the wall partitions of their homes.[15]

---

10. Allen and Leonard, *Story*, 536–37.
11. As quoted in Gibbons, 179.
12. As quoted in Gibbons, 179.
13. Gibbons, 180.
14. As noted by Quinn, *Elder Statesman: A Biography of J. Reuben Clark* (Salt Lake City: Signature Books, 2002), 99.
15. Gibbons, 180, 182.

LDS officials responded in other ways. Lee wrote on December 19 that Clark asked him to "submit names of leading younger men for membership on air raid committees now being organized in the city." Beginning in January 1942, church leaders ceased calling young men to missionary service. Conscription-related requirements meant that missionary calls were extended only to sisters, older men, and the physically disabled.[16] Also beginning in April 1942, and continuing for the duration of the war, the church's semi-annual general conference was closed to the general membership, confined to approximately 500 male priesthood leaders. Also, due to paper shortages, the publication of instruction manuals and other materials was severely limited.[17]

Over the course of World War II, nearly 100,000 young LDS men and women served in all branches of the US armed forces. In response, church leaders formed the LDS Servicemen's Committee in October 1942. Lee was placed in charge, assisted by Hugh B. Brown, who over the previous year had served as LDS servicemen's coordinator, attending to the needs and concerns of the increasing numbers of young LDS men in the military.[18] Over the following three years, from 1942 to 1945, Lee and Brown enjoyed a close working relationship while operating the committee.

Brown, some seventeen years older than Lee, boasted a varied record of accomplishments both in the United States and Canada. He was born in Granger, Utah, in 1883. His father, a farmer, moved the family to western Canada when Hugh was young. Upon coming of age, Brown returned to Utah to attend college and, following that, filled a missionary calling in Great Britain under mission president Heber J. Grant. Following his return, Brown married his childhood sweetheart, Zina Young Card, and together they moved to Canada in 1906 where they remained for the next two decades. In the process, Brown become a Canadian citizen, holding dual US–Canadian citizenship. Brown ultimately settled on a career in law. He served as president of the Lethbridge Stake in Canada prior to returning to Utah in 1927. Settling in Salt Lake City, he continued his law

---

16. Gibbons, 181.
17. Allen and Leonard, *Story,* 539.
18. Allen and Leonard, *Story,* 540–41.

career as a partner with the firm of J. Reuben Clark, Albert Bowen, and Preston D. Richards. His subsequent church service included presiding over the British Mission. Brown's extensive church service, combined with his record as an officer in the Canadian Military Reserves for some five years during World War I, rendered him ideal to work with Lee in overseeing the LDS Servicemen's Committee.[19]

The Servicemen's Committee assumed responsibility for providing church programs and guidelines to Latter-day Saints in the military and for securing government cooperation in the appointment of LDS chaplains for all branches of the armed forces. A second charge involved allowing LDS servicemen to have "LDS" rather than "Protestant" stamped on their dog tags.[20]

Under Lee's direction, the Servicemen's Committee implemented a special publications program, resulting in the printing of directories containing maps and church addresses worldwide. Also produced for LDS military personnel were pocket-sized editions of the Book of Mormon and a church book entitled *Principles of the Gospel*. Each LDS military person was provided copies of the monthly *Improvement Era* magazine and the weekly Church News section of the *Deseret News*.[21]

Both Lee and Brown, in conjunction with their responsibilities with the Servicemen's Committee, visited various military bases and installations along the West Coast. On occasion the pair was accompanied by Apostle Albert Bowen, likewise a member of the Servicemen's Committee.

On one memorable occasion, while visiting a facility in Portland, Oregon, in August 1942, the traveling church officials were reminded of the grim realities of war when Brown received a copy of the memorial service held for his son who had been killed while flying for the Royal Air Force in Great Britain.[22] Both Lee and Bowen were so impressed with Brown's role in handling his duties that they

---

19. For two perspectives on the career of Hugh B. Brown, see Eugene E. Campbell and Richard Poll, *Hugh B. Brown: His Life and Thought* (Salt Lake City: Bookcraft, 1975), and Edwin B. Firmage, ed., *An Abundant Life: The Memoirs of Hugh B. Brown* (Salt Lake City: Signature Books, 1999).

20. Allen and Leonard, *Story,* 541.

21. Allen and Leonard, *Story,* 542.

22. Gibbons, 183–87.

recommended he "be given General Authority status as an Assistant to the Twelve."[23] Though this did not happen at the time, Brown was eventually named an assistant to the Twelve in October 1953.

*

Throughout the 1940s and 1950s, Lee tackled other important matters, often working closely with J. Reuben Clark.

Clark was compelled to assume a gradually greater role in overseeing church affairs given Heber J. Grant's precarious health in the wake of his 1940 stroke. From 1940 to 1945, Clark "was often the only member of the First Presidency at the office for weeks or months at a time."[24] Further complicating matters, Grant initially insisted on carrying on with his duties. This, however, soon proved counterproductive and further eroded his physical condition. By April 1942, Grant was so weak that he was unable to speak at subsequent general conferences. A year later, his health had declined to the point that he was unable to attend the regular weekly meetings of the First Presidency and Quorum of the Twelve.[25] Indeed, Grant "was virtually bedridden during the mid-1940s."[26] Thus "J. Reuben Clark was the de facto President of the Church, and President Grant not only knew it, but allowed it."[27]

Clark sought ways to improve the efficiency of the church in its administrative operations. In April 1941, acting in consultation with David O. McKay, Clark authorized the creation of a new category of apostles, called Assistants to the Twelve. The responsibility of these assistants was to aid the current Quorum of the Twelve in assuming the "added burdens of travel and administration."[28] The first five assistants called were Marion G. Romney, Thomas E. McKay, Clifford E. Young, Alma Sonne, and Nicholas G. Smith. All five were ordained at the same time that Lee was ordained an apostle. Two of the five, Romney and Smith, were "close personal and social friends of Elder and Sister Lee."[29]

---

23. Gibbons, 187.
24. As noted by Quinn, *Elder Statesman*, 92.
25. Quinn, *Elder Statesman*, 100.
26. Quinn, *Elder Statesman*, 91.
27. As noted by A. Hamer Reiser, in Quinn, *Elder Statesman*, 100.
28. Quinn, *Elder Statesman*, 96.
29. Goates, 164.

Shortly thereafter, Clark took Lee into his confidence to discuss the need for "a simplification of the present Church programs." Clark proposed implementing a "Memorandum of Suggestions" he had drafted, calling on the heads of the various church auxiliary organizations—the Mutual Improvement Association (MIA), Relief Society, the Primary, and the Sunday school—to "coordinate and streamline their activities and instructional manuals." Clark's plan was not implemented, primarily due to strong opposition from the auxiliary groups, all of which feared the loss of autonomy and independence. But for Lee, "the concepts sank deep into [his] fertile mind," serving as the basis for his own future proposals for church correlation, implemented years later.[30]

Clark conferred with Lee on yet another important matter two years later. This involved the filling of two vacancies that opened in the Quorum of the Twelve following the deaths of Sylvester Q. Cannon and Rudger Clawson in 1943. As Lee recalled, "We discussed the names of Spencer W. Kimball and Ezra Taft Benson … I was pleased to know that President Grant had already decided to appoint one or the other of these two, or probably both, inasmuch as they had both been in my mind as the logical men to appoint."[31] Such a response is not surprising given that Lee had enjoyed "favorable contacts" with the two men during the course of recent travels for the church, first, to Duncan, Arizona, where Kimball served as stake president, and later to Washington, DC, where Benson held the same position overseeing the Washington, DC Stake.[32] Lee, moreover, had known Benson since childhood. Later that same year, both Kimball and Benson were ordained as members of the Twelve at the October 1943 general conference.

That same year, Clark enlisted Lee's assistance in dealing with an extramarital affair involving Apostle Richard Lyman. Lyman was a senior member of the Twelve, having been appointed in 1918 by President Joseph F. Smith. In mid-October 1943, Clark took Lee into his confidence, asking him to begin a secret inquiry. Following that, Clark and Lee began surveilling Lyman, who could be seen

---

30. Quinn, *Elder Statesman*, 98.
31. As quoted in Gibbons, 200.
32. Gibbons, 199.

frequenting the apartment of a woman he had known for several years. Clark and Lee informed church president Heber J. Grant of their findings. At Clark's direction, Lee and Apostle Joseph Fielding Smith accompanied members of the Salt Lake City police department to forcibly enter the woman's apartment, catching the couple in a compromising relationship. In a November 1943 trial convened by the Twelve, Lyman was stripped of his apostleship and excommunicated from the church.[33]

Several factors made the Lyman affair noteworthy. First, Lyman hailed from a prominent LDS family. His father, Francis M. Lyman, and grandfather, Amasa M. Lyman, also served as apostles. Richard Lyman was extremely well educated, having earned degrees from the University of Michigan, University of Chicago, and Cornell University. Lyman's wife, Amy Brown Lyman, was herself a high-ranking church officer, general president of the Relief Society. The affair revealed lingering elements of Mormon fundamentalist polygamy—a rapidly emerging movement that LDS Church officials were attempting to stamp out. The woman had been involved in an earlier unauthorized polygamous marriage. Lyman may have looked to polygamy to justify his transgression, but the church court rejected any such explanation and Lyman was officially expelled for "violation of the Christian law of chastity." Recalling the trial and its conclusion, Lee lamented: "It was a most saddening experience, with most of the Twelve in tears as Brother Lyman was asked to leave the meeting and shook hands with each brother in parting those sacred premises and that choice companionship for the last time."[34]

Taking Lyman's place was Mark E. Petersen, ordained to the Twelve in April 1944. Petersen, born and raised in Salt Lake City, attended the University of Utah, after which he pursued a career in journalism. He rose through the ranks of LDS Church-owned *Deseret News*, starting as a reporter and ultimately becoming the paper's president and board chair. Petersen was forty-three years old at the

---

33. Quinn, *Elder Statesman*, 252.

34. As recalled by Lee, in Goates, 185. For a scholarly historical analysis of Lyman's excommunication, see Gary James Bergera, "Transgressions in the Latter-day Saint Community: The Cases of Albert Carrington, Richard R. Lyman, and Joseph F. Smith. Part II: Richard R. Lyman," *Journal of Mormon History* 37, no. 4 (Fall 2011): 173–207.

time of his calling as an apostle.[35] Lee responded positively to the Petersen's appointment, noting that the "choice was well received … the selection of one of his background … and his age seemed appreciated by everyone."[36] Lee, in fact, had previously recommended the youthful newspaperman as a potential appointee to the Twelve.[37]

*

Over the two-year period from 1943 to 1945, Lee took on an array of additional responsibilities. In July 1943, he was appointed as an advisor to church's General Primary Board. Marion G. Romney was likewise appointed. Together, the men worked closely with the three-member Primary board offering suggestions. In early 1944, Lee assumed chairmanship of a special committee established to produce a new, updated hymnal—the assignment coming as a result of his own musical background.[38]

Also in 1944, Lee was called to serve on the newly formed Church Publication Committee, chaired by senior apostles Joseph Fielding Smith and John A. Widtsoe. This committee was assigned to review and approve all church publications. Lee's major assignment during this period was chairing the Melchizedek Priesthood Committee.[39]

At the beginning of 1945, Lee received a different type of assignment—one that proved challenging in a different way. The First Presidency asked him to give a series of Sunday-evening lectures on church-owned radio station KSL. Entitled "Youth and the Church," Lee's twenty-four one-hour lectures were presented over a six-month period from January through June 1945.

The lectures dealt with a broad spectrum of doctrinal issues. Their preparation proved time-consuming for the already-busy apostle. As Lee noted in his diary, "Spent the day [Saturday] entirely locked up in the office at the Church Office Building trying to get some inspiration to make some preparations for the … radio talks."[40] He drew on his life experiences as a teacher in public schools and the Church

35. For an overview of Petersen's life, see Peggy Peterson Burton, *Mark E. Petersen: A Biography* (Salt Lake City: Deseret Book Co., 1985).

36. Lee, as quoted in Goates, 183.

37. As noted in Gibbons, 201.

38. Gibbons, 183.

39. Gibbons, 183.

40. As noted by Lee, in Goates, 186.

Education System, as well as his experience as a tutor of young missionaries preparing for church service.[41] He also sought advice and insights from his own daughters who were young adults by this time, aged nineteen and twenty. The grateful father acknowledged, "My own daughters, Maurine and Helen, served as representatives of the modern youth of the day, and were my chief critics and consultants."[42]

Such preparation notwithstanding, Lee's radio presentations received a mixed response among LDS faithful. Some listeners "thought he used too many scriptures, some said his applications of the scriptural lessons came too late … and some said it wasn't entertaining enough. One statement was universal. Everyone seemed to feel that Elder Lee had issued a challenge that was going to be difficult for the youth to meet."[43]

Also weighing in was the apostle's mentor and associate, J. Reuben Clark. As Lee recalled following one of his radio addresses, "President Clark called to commend me. He has been very kind and his constant encouragement has been a source of great strength."[44] Yet on occasion, Clark offered his own corrections when he felt his protégé had erred. Clark presented such a critique following Lee's "Youth of a Noble Birthright" address, defending the controversial doctrine of priesthood denial and temple ban on black people.[45] As recalled by Lee, "President Clark thought I was just a little severe in my treatment of the negroes and the curse placed on them [but also] agreed entirely with my doctrine and gave me some suggestions for the paragraph relating to the negroes and intermarriage with them."[46] On another occasion, Clark allegedly "told Brother Lee that some of the General Authorities thought he was speaking too plainly about some of the principles of the gospel." Clark himself went on to reassure Lee, "If you pleased your critics, you wouldn't please me."[47]

---

41. Gibbons, 215.

42. As quoted in Harold B. Lee, *Youth and the Church* (Salt Lake City: Deseret News Press, 1945), iii.

43. As quoted in Goates, 187.

44. As recalled by Lee, in Goates, 187.

45. Lee's "Youth of a Noble Birthright" was subsequently published in his *Youth and the Church*, 167–76.

46. As noted in Harold B. Lee, diary, entries for May 7 and 8, 1945, as recorded in typescript kept by L. Brent Goates. Copy courtesy of Reid Moon.

47. As noted in Goates, 187.

The controversial aspects of Lee's "Youth and the Church" sermons notwithstanding, they generated significant attention among the LDS faithful, particularly after they subsequently appeared in the Church News section of the *Deseret News*. Following that, the individual addresses were issued as pamphlets and distributed throughout the church. Ultimately the twenty-four lectures were gathered together into a book published in late 1945 under the title *Youth and the Church*. In the volume's foreword, Lee's fellow apostle and close associate Ezra Taft Benson effused: "Both young and old will find in this volume safe answers to perplexing problems of companionship, courtship, marriage, homebuilding, everyday choices of right and wrong, ideals, and the basic factors which determine success and happiness."[48] *Youth and the Church* secured for Lee his well-earned reputation as an articulate, outspoken proponent of orthodox LDS doctrine and practices, generally of a conservative bent.

As a proponent of LDS orthodoxy, Lee, along with fellow general authorities, reacted with alarm and anger to Fawn McKay Brodie's biography of Joseph Smith, *No Man Knows My History*, published in November 1945.[49] Throughout the pages of her controversial, naturalistic biography of Smith, Brodie characterized the church founder as "a conscious fraud." Her biography generated widespread attention from both within and outside of the LDS community. Brodie hailed from a prominent Latter-day Saint family; her father, Thomas E. McKay, was an assistant to the Twelve, and her uncle David O. McKay was second counselor in the First Presidency.[50]

LDS general authorities reacted quickly to condemn the "Brodie book," with church president George Albert Smith leading the way. To an audience of the faithful gathered for the April 1946 general conference, Smith, without mentioning the author by name, declared, "There have been some who have belittled [Joseph Smith] but I would like to say that those who have done so will be forgotten and their remains will go back to mother earth … and the odor of their infamy will never die." Lee, upon reading the biography, dismissed it as "another defilement

---

48. Ezra Taft Benson, "Foreword," to Lee, *Youth and the Church*, viii.

49. Fawn M. Brodie, *No Man Knows My History: The Life of Joseph Smith* (New York: Alfred A. Knopf, 1945); a second edition, revised and enlarged, appeared in 1970.

50. For a discussion of Brodie, see Newell G. Bringhurst, *Fawn McKay Brodie: A Biographer's Life* (Norman: University of Oklahoma Press, 1999).

of sacred things." He condemned "those who sought to gain fame and fortune by demeaning the Prophet Joseph Smith."[51]

Brodie was subsequently charged with "apostasy," tried, convicted, and excommunicated by a bishop's court in Cambridge, Massachusetts, in June 1946. Orders for her excommunication appear to have come from her uncle David O. McKay.[52]

*

Aside from Lee's emergence as a prominent church spokesman, the year 1945 was marked by other important changes affecting not just the LDS Church but society at large. Most significantly, the fighting of World War II drew to a close, first in Europe with the surrender of Nazi Germany in May 1945, and then three months later in the Pacific with the surrender of Japan following the dropping of A-bombs that obliterated the cities of Hiroshima and Nagasaki.

Among the one hundred thousand LDS military personnel who fought for the United States, five thousand lost their lives. Among the Latter-day Saints who survived was future apostle Neal A. Maxwell, who, as a US Army infantryman, fought in the battle for Okinawa and was part of the post-war occupation force in Japan. Often forgotten is that Latter-day Saints fought on both sides of the conflict. Some seven hundred German Latter-day Saints, primarily soldiers, died as result of the war.[53]

Lee took charge of two important post-war church-related activities. First, as chair of the Church Military Relations Committee, he supervised the process of helping returning LDS servicemen transition back to civilian life. He oversaw the development of support services and programs for veterans.[54]

Second, in his role as welfare department director, Lee oversaw the delivery of relief to those European Latter-day Saints left devastated by the war. Lee worked with fellow apostle Ezra Taft Benson, then-president of the European Mission, in the distribution of food, clothing, and other commodities. Also aiding in this process was

---

51. Lee, in Goates, 197.

52. See Bringhurst, *Fawn McKay Brodie,* 113, for McKay's role in Brodie's excommunication.

53. Robert C. Freeman and Dennis A. Wright, eds., *Saints at War: Memories of LDS Soldiers in World War II* (Salt Lake City: Covenant Communications, 2001).

54. Gibbons, 216, 227.

Marion G. Romney. In all, some thirteen railway cars of food and five cars of clothing were shipped to Europe and distributed.[55]

*

Affecting the church as a whole was a change in leadership following the death of long-serving president Heber J. Grant in May 1945. Replacing Grant was seventy-five-year-old George Albert Smith. Hailing from Mormonism's most prominent family, Smith was the grandnephew of Joseph Smith Sr. and grandson of George A. Smith—a prominent nineteenth-century apostle. George Albert Smith himself was a long-serving apostle, appointed in 1903. Smith, however, was frail in physical constitution, plus he suffered from "mental trouble" or, more bluntly, periodic episodes of "mental collapse," which had incapacitated him for a period of time years earlier. Although Smith recovered, he continued to suffer symptoms in the 1930s and into his tenure as church president.[56]

Sensitive to Smith's physical and mental condition, J. Reuben Clark sought to assist the "frail and elderly" church leader as much as possible. This proved challenging, given that Smith possessed a "workaholic disposition," thus often attempting to do more than he perhaps should have. Moreover, Smith was influenced by his strong-willed daughter, Emily Smith Stewart, who sometimes championed her own agenda.[57]

By the fall of 1948, Smith had driven himself so relentlessly that he was on the verge of another nervous breakdown. His condition worsened over the next year to the point that he was briefly hospitalized with what was described as "tired nerves." Thus, he was compelled to scale back his activities. By 1950, a further decline in health resulted in more absences from his duties. He found some rest and respite in Laguna Beach and Hawaii. Nonetheless, Smith insisted on carrying out his official responsibilities, albeit with decreasing effectiveness as "the distractions of illness and old age slowed his comprehension or caused forgetfulness."[58]

*

Clark eventually found himself again assuming a central role in

55. Goates, 197–99; Gibbons, 226–29.

56. Richard S. Van Wagoner and Steven C. Walker, "George Albert Smith," *A Book of Mormons* (Salt Lake City: Signature Books, 1982), 275–81.

57. Quinn, *Elder Statesman*, 109–11.

58. Quinn, *Elder Statesman*, 124–28.

overseeing church affairs. At the same time, Clark consulted closely with David O. McKay and the Council of the Twelve, including Lee.

Concurrently, Lee emerged as an increasingly dominant figure among the Twelve. He moved up in seniority as three new apostles were ordained during the late 1940s.

The first of the three, Matthew Cowley, was called in October 1945 to fill a vacancy created by the elevation of George Albert Smith to church president. Cowley, born in Preston, Idaho, in 1907, was the son of one-time apostle Matthias Cowley. The family moved to Salt Lake City where Matthew came of age, attended and graduated from the University of Utah, and subsequently attended George Washington University, where he received a law degree. He presided over the New Zealand Mission from 1938 to 1945.[59]

Two years later, Henry D. Moyle was elevated to the apostleship to take the place of eighty-year-old Charles Callis, who died in January 1947. Moyle, a longtime associate of Lee, had presided over the Cottonwood Stake and chaired the Church Welfare Committee.[60]

The third, Delbert L. Stapley, was called to the Twelve in October 1950, replacing long-serving senior apostle and president of the Twelve, eighty-nine-year-old George F. Richards, who died the previous August. Stapley was born in Mesa, Arizona, in 1896. As a youth, he demonstrated talent as a baseball player, but turned down a chance to play major league baseball in favor of church service. He subsequently served an LDS mission in the southern United States. Following that, he served as a US Marine in World War II. Involved in municipal politics, he sat on the Mesa City Council and lobbied for the development of the Colorado River water system. He was president of the Phoenix Arizona Stake prior to his elevation to the apostleship.[61]

The three new apostles were all relatively young when compared to their predecessors. The youngest, Cowley, was just forty-eight years old at the time of his ordination. All three, together with

---

59. Henry A. Smith, *Matthew Cowley: A Man of Faith* (Salt Lake City: Utah Printing Co., 1954).

60. Richard D. Poll, *Working the Divine Miracle: The Life of Apostle Henry D. Moyle*, ed. Stan Larson (Salt Lake City: Signature Books, 1999).

61. "Death of Elder Delbert Stapley Mourned," *Ensign*, Oct. 1978, reprint of *Deseret News* obituary, Oct. 20, 1978.

Lee, Kimball, Benson, and Petersen, constituted a majority bloc of seven young, vigorous, dedicated general authorities actively shaping church policy and doctrine. Lee assumed a dominant role in the group, given his apostolic seniority and strong, take-charge demeanor. This earned him the title, "Dean of the Younger Apostles."

*

Lee, meanwhile, continued to focus on his assignments as directed by the First Presidency. The most important was oversight of the Church Welfare Program. In 1946 the welfare program faced a major crisis resulting from a US presidential order directing the Department of Agriculture to seize all excess grain in storage at various facilities, including those owned by the church. If carried out, this order "would cripple the Church's wheat storage program." Thus, Lee traveled to Washington, DC, to meet with government officials. Ultimately the outstanding issues were resolved, and the church wheat storage program was allowed to continue. On a second trip to the nation's capital in May 1950, Lee secured tax-exempt status for Deseret Industries—an important arm of the Church Welfare Program.[62]

Lee presided over a significant expansion of the welfare program through the procurement of large parcels of land in both California and Florida. In 1950 the church negotiated the purchase of over 1,000 acres of farmland in Parris, California, seventy miles east southeast of Los Angeles. Subsequently, a regional welfare farm was established under the direction of the ten LDS stakes in the region. Soon the church secured an even larger parcel of land, some 54,000 acres near Orlando, Florida. This huge tract was obtained through the efforts of Henry D. Moyle. The acreage, initially designed as a cattle ranch, eventually expanded to over 300,000 acres, making it the largest cattle ranch in the United States. Farming on the land was expanded to include citrus. The entire facility came to be known as Deseret Cattle and Citrus Ranch.[63]

Meanwhile, in 1947, Lee, Stephen L. Richards, and Albert E. Bowen were assigned to a special committee of the Twelve to consider the need for correlation, specifically the consolidation of greater priesthood control over church auxiliaries. The call for organizational

62. Goates, 225–27.
63. Goates, 227–28.

efficiency was driven by church expansion within the United States and abroad during the post-World-War-II period. Total church membership increased from 892,000 in 1941 to 1,147,000 in 1951. This represented an increase of some 255,000 new members. The annual rate of church growth thus doubled from 2 percent before World War II to 4 percent during the postwar period.

The correlation committee found that the auxiliaries, especially the Relief Society, Mutual Improvement Association (MIA), and Primary Association, had become so powerful as to almost function as independent entities. Each prepared, approved, and published its own instructional materials. Each had its own budget. All had large general boards whose members traveled extensively to hold separate training sessions with local church leaders, effectively independent from any input from local priesthood leaders.[64]

To remedy the situation, the correlation committee recommended that all the auxiliaries be brought under direct, centralized priesthood direction. The committee further called for local priesthood leaders to assume greater authority and responsibility for auxiliary activities and the training of auxiliary leaders within their domain. The intention was to "greatly diminish the authority and status of the general auxiliary executives and the boards."[65]

The committee's recommendations received strong support from First Presidency counselors J. Reuben Clark and David O. McKay. However, the recommended reforms met with strong resistance from the auxiliaries directly affected. This caused Lee to lament, "It seems doubtful the time is here for much modification in our present programs because of sentimental objections."[66] Most important, President George Albert Smith strongly opposed the proposed reforms, which delayed their eventual implementation.[67]

*

Throughout this period, Lee maintained a close working and personal relationship with Reuben Clark. The older man frequently imparted counsel on both official and personal matters. Periodically,

---

64. Gibbons, 250–51.
65. Gibbons, 251.
66. Lee, as quoted in Gibbons, 252.
67. Gibbons, 252.

he briefed Lee on policy matters outside the scope of his responsibility. Moreover, Clark would occasionally use Lee to float ideas in church committee meetings, ideas Clark did not want to have seen as originating from him.[68]

Indeed, the two men went even further in expressing their admiration for one another. As Lee recalled on one occasion, Clark "said he loved me as his own son and that I had returned and reciprocated that love as a son to a father."[69] Lee further declared on another occasion that Clark "has been a real father to me."[70] Lee, in responding to Clark's compliment, admitted, "There was nothing more that I desired than to please him [Clark] and my Heavenly Father."[71]

As previously noted, both men emerged from lower-middle-class LDS families, though each had chosen wives from prominent LDS families. Moreover, each man's wife strongly influenced her husband.[72]

Clark, aware that his and Lee's forebearers came from less-than-prominent backgrounds, alluded to this fact in an LDS general conference address delivered in October 1947 in conjunction with the centennial observance of the Mormons' arrival in the Great Salt Lake Valley. Clark's "To Them of the Last Wagon" criticized the tendency by church leaders to focus exclusively on the contributions of prominent pioneers and their descendants, while minimizing or ignoring the role played by the common folk. Clark scolded the descendants of prominent families for basking in the reflected glory of their ancestors.[73] Not surprisingly, Lee praised Clark's speech as a "protest to the church aristocracy that some name families have seemed to feel." He agreed fully with Clark's observation "that the descendants of some of the early Mormon leaders might succumb to the folly of the Jews at the time of Christ who asserted superiority over others merely because they were descendants of Abraham."[74]

Further facilitating Lee's attraction to Clark as a surrogate father was the limited interaction he had with his own father, Samuel. The

---

68. Gibbons, 264.
69. Lee, in Goates, 178.
70. Lee, in Goates, 177.
71. Lee, in Gibbons, 201.
72. See Quinn, *Elder Statesman*, esp. 1–25.
73. Quinn, *Elder Statesman*, 118–19.
74. Lee, in Gibbons, 250.

elder Lee never completely recovered from the trauma of his expulsion from the church years earlier. Although Samuel, along with Harold's mother, Louisa, ultimately settled in Salt Lake City, living in close proximity to their increasingly prominent son, interactions between father and son remained sporadic. Meanwhile, Samuel supported himself and his wife as a night supervisor at the ZCMI department store. Samuel Lee died of heart and kidney failure on May 9, 1947, at age seventy-one.[75]

Meanwhile, Harold and Fern's two daughters continued their education. Helen attended the University of Utah, and Maurine Brigham Young University. Both married shortly after graduating. Helen exchanged nuptials with Lesley Brent Goates on June 24, 1946, in the Salt Lake Temple, with her father officiating. Lee described the event as "one of the greatest experiences of my life."[76] Goates was born and raised in Salt Lake City. After graduating from the University of Utah, he spent a dozen years in journalism. He subsequently became a hospital administrator, overseeing the LDS church's multi-hospital system as assistant commissioner. He and Helen had six children.[77]

A year later, on June 11, 1947, the Lees' oldest daughter, Maureen, married Ernest J. Wilkins in a ceremony performed by her father likewise in the Salt Lake Temple. Maureen and Ernest met and courted while at BYU. Wilkins, a native of Franklin, Arizona, served an LDS mission to Argentina and was a World War II veteran. Wounded in combat, he was subsequently awarded a Purple Heart. After graduating from Stanford University with a PhD, Wilkins became a professor of languages and cultural studies first at BYU and then at the University of Utah. Following a career in teaching, he served as president of the LDS Language Training Mission (LTM) from 1961 to 1970. He and Maureen became the parents of four children.[78]

In July 1949, the Lees sold their two-story home in west Salt Lake City and moved to an apartment on 106 First Avenue in downtown

---

75. Goates, 211–12.

76. Lee, in Gibbons, 199.

77. See "About the Author" in Goates. Also see "L. Brent Goates," Obituary, *Deseret News*, Nov. 23, 2016.

78. "Ernest J. Wilkins," at www.findagrave.com/memorial/76562037/ernest-j-wikins.

Salt Lake City—a short distance from Harold's office in the Church Administration Building. Prompting the move was Fern's increasing difficulty in keeping up and maintaining the house due to her health problems, which continued to worsen.[79] In March 1950 she suffered a bowel hemorrhage and required hospitalization.[80]

Lee struggled with health problems of his own. As early as May 1945, his physician informed him that he showed signs of chronic physical fatigue, reflected in a "rapid pulse rate and low blood pressure"—considered unusual for a man his age. He was forty-six years old.[81]

Lee's hectic church schedule was clearly taking its toll. Particularly arduous were his regular out-of-town trips, sometimes over extended periods of time, to preside over stake conferences. In March 1947, the ever-busy apostle suffered chronic chest pains—a warning that he was overworking himself.[82] But Lee was not inclined to slow down. "Working under pressure and fatigue seemed Harold B. Lee's lot throughout his ministry," wrote son-in-law Brent Goates, adding it was "almost as if there were not enough time to accomplish his life's mission."[83]

*

Lee's health problems notwithstanding, he could look back on the 1940s as a period of accomplishment for himself and for the church he loved and served. Under his supervision, the Church Welfare Program extended its humanitarian relief to European Saints suffering the ravages of World War II, while also expanding its reach in the United States. Lee also presented himself as a vigorous proponent of orthodox church doctrine and practice. Equally significant, he established his place as a dominant voice in the Quorum of the Twelve by virtue of his swift assent from junior to senior apostle.

79. Goates, 180.
80. Goates, 230.
81. Goates, 187–88.
82. Goates, 212.
83. As quoted by the author himself, in Goates, 216.

CHAPTER SIX

A CHANGING CHURCH

1951-61

The year 1951, marking the ten-year anniversary of Lee's tenure as a general authority, represented a significant milestone, both for the apostle and the church as a whole. The passing of President George Albert Smith in 1951 led to David O. McKay's becoming the church's ninth prophet-president. Under McKay's administration, significant changes occurred within the church and the larger world. Lee played an increasingly important role in such changes.

*

The death of George Albert Smith on April 4, 1951, at age eighty-one, was not unexpected; the ailing leader had been in critical condition for some two months previously.[1]

Smith's successor, David Oman McKay, stood in sharp contrast to his predecessor.[2] McKay appeared both "vigorous and well-preserved" despite being a mere three years younger than the frail Smith. McKay, by contrast, was impressive in physical appearance, with a large frame, standing six feet one inch. An admiring non-Mormon journalist noted that McKay's "massive, well-groomed mane of white hair tops a handsome face that shines with strong character."[3] Indeed, the charismatic McKay, donning a distinctive white suit, presented "an affable new image of Mormonism to a world that had previously seen Mormon leaders as dour, suited figures."[4]

---

1. Goates, 237–39.

2. A good biography of McKay is Gregory A. Prince and Wm Robert Wright, *David O. McKay and the Rise of Modern Mormonism* (Salt Lake City: University of Utah Press, 2005).

3. As later quoted in Terry W. Call, "David O. McKay," Church News section of the *Deseret News*, September 25, 1993.

4. "Prophet, Seer, and Innovator," *Time,* February 1970, 50.

McKay boasted an impressive background prior to being called to the apostleship in 1906 at the age of thirty-two. As a member of the Weber Stake School Board of Education, he inaugurated a number of teaching and curriculum reforms. He implemented a similar program of reform following his call to the apostleship. McKay's vision of the international potential of Mormonism was shaped by his year-long tour of LDS missions throughout the world in 1920 and subsequent tenure as president of the church's European Mission from 1922 to 1924. From 1933 to 1951, he served as second counselor in the First Presidencies of Heber J. Grant and George Albert Smith.[5]

Upon being sustained as president, McKay reorganized the First Presidency. In a shocking move, he selected as his first counselor Stephen L. Richards, thereby demoting second counselor J. Reuben Clark, his long-time associate in the First Presidency. McKay's action stunned not only Clark, but the other members of the Twelve. Among the quorum, "there was numbing silence" along with "overwhelming sympathy for President Clark."[6] Lee was particularly dismayed by the demotion of his mentor and surrogate father. Upon visiting Clark immediately afterwards, Lee found "him humble, yet loyal to President McKay." According to Lee, Clark "assured me that he would … try his best to be a good counselor, despite the humiliation that was inescapable." Clark further stated he "would seek … an explanation as to why such a change in the order of councilors."[7]

McKay stated that his decision to demote Clark was based on "apostolic seniority" since Richards had been ordained an apostle in 1917, Clark in 1933. McKay further explained that Richards was "his closest friend" among the general authorities.[8]

McKay's rejection of Clark was driven by other factors. While McKay denied "any rift," the two men clearly clashed both in personality and leadership style. In temperament, McKay was open

---

5. Prince and Wright, *David O. McKay*, 5–10. Also see Newell G. Bringhurst, "The Private versus Public David O. McKay: Profile of a Complex Personality," in *Dimensions of Faith: A Mormon Studies Reader*, ed. Stephen C. Taysom (Salt Lake City: Signature Books, 2011), 1–24.

6. Goates, 239.

7. Lee, as quoted in Goates, 239.

8. D. Michael Quinn, *Elder Statesman: A Biography of J. Reuben Clark* (Salt Lake City: Signature Books, 2002), 144.

and optimistic, asserting that "man's character was basically good," whereas Clark "was an unreconstructed pessimist." In administering church affairs, McKay "favored expansive growth and more liberal expenditure of funds, whereas Clark "favored slow growth and cautious expenditure of funds." In decision-making, McKay tended "to make immediate decisions based on personal impressions," while Clark demanded "thorough research" prior to rendering a decision.[9]

New First Counselor Richards differed from Clark both in heritage and experiences. Richards was born in 1879 in Mendon, Utah, the oldest of ten children to Stephen Longstroth Richards and Emma Louise Stayner. Boasting a patrician LDS background, Richards was the grandson of early church leader Willard Richards. The younger Richards had trained as a lawyer, graduating from the University of Chicago with a JD. Following graduation, he returned to Salt Lake City to practice law and teach at the University of Utah. Richards's close relationship with McKay commenced following his elevation to the Twelve. The pair served together on the Deseret Sunday School Union; Richards also served under McKay during the latter's tenure as the church's Commissioner of Education. Through their close working relationship, they became good friends. As a token of their warm friendship, Richards purchased for McKay and the church the iconic *Christus* statue, which was subsequently placed in the visitors' center on Temple Square.

Lee responded positively to Richards's elevation to the First Presidency, the unprecedented circumstances surrounding his appointment notwithstanding. Lee had, in fact, enjoyed a congenial working relationship with Richards during the latter's tenure as a senior apostle. Lee fondly recalled Richards's role as mentor: "His counsel was wise and timely and his procedure was an excellent training for me," further noting his "deep spiritual sense, which occasionally seemed to be obscured by his high intellect."[10]

Lee had worked with Richards on a special committee to develop plans for a churchwide "simplification program to give more emphasis to the Priesthood."[11] Richards was anxious to move forward

---

9. As quoted by Quinn, *Elder Statesman*, 136–37.
10. Lee, as quoted in Gibbons, 288.
11. Goates, 366.

with the program but was prevented from doing so given the lack of support from McKay, whose more immediate focus was promoting the expansion of the LDS Church within the United States and especially abroad.[12]

*

Meanwhile, Lee continued to move up in terms of seniority in the Twelve. Shifts in the membership of the Quorum of the Twelve also occurred, which further enhanced Lee's status. In October 1951, Lee's longtime close associate on the welfare committee Marion G. Romney was called to the apostleship to fill the vacancy created by elevation of Stephen L. Richards. "Needless to say," Lee commented, "my joy is unbounded at his [Romney's] coming into the Council."[13]

Over the next two years, four members of the Twelve passed away. Joseph F Merrill, an apostle since 1931, died in February 1952. Appointed to replace him was LeGrand Richards, the son of former longtime apostle George F. Richards. The younger Richards was descended from one of Mormonism's leading pioneer families. His grandfather, Franklin D. Richards, had also served as a Mormon apostle. LeGrand Richards himself boasted a long record of church service, his most recent calling being that of presiding bishop.[14]

In November 1952, a second senior apostle, John A. Widtsoe, passed away at age eighty. Replacing Widtsoe was Adam S. Bennion, ordained to the Twelve in April 1953. Bennion, like Widtsoe, was an academic, having served on the Deseret Sunday School Board and on the church's Board of Education prior to his ordination at age sixty-six.

Yet a third senior member of the Twelve, seventy-seven-year-old Albert E. Bowen, died in July 1953. Appointed to replace him was Richard L. Evans, who, at age forty-seven, was sustained in October 1953. Despite his relative youth, Evans was a familiar figure to the LDS faithful as the host and announcer for the weekly Mormon Tabernacle Choir radio broadcast, *Music and the Spoken Word.* He also served as the narrator for many church films, most notably *Man's Search for Happiness.*[15]

---

12. Gibbons, 288–89.

13. Lee, as quoted in Gibbons, 290.

14. Lucile Tate, *LeGrand Richards: Beloved Apostle* (Salt Lake City: Bookcraft, 1982).

15. Richard L. Evans Jr., *Richard L. Evans: The Man and the Message* (Salt Lake City: Bookcraft, 1973).

Apostle Matthew Cowley died suddenly in December 1953 at fifty-six years old. Replacing him was eighty-year-old George Q. Morris, ordained to the Twelve in April 1954. Morris had the dubious distinction of being the oldest person in church history to be elevated to the apostleship. Prior to his ordination, Morris had served as superintendent of the Young Men's Mutual Improvement Association and as an assistant to the Twelve.

One other noteworthy change within the Twelve involved the temporary leave of absence of Apostle Ezra Taft Benson in January 1953 to serve as US Secretary of Agriculture in the administration of President Dwight D. Eisenhower. McKay supported Benson's new calling "out of a sense of obligation to the country." McKay also believed that having an apostle at the center of the federal government "would have a beneficial effect" on both the country and the church, greatly enhancing the latter's image.[16]

Lee conveyed his "genuine congratulations" at the "significant recognition" brought to Benson and the church.[17] He endorsed Benson's controversial farm policy reforms, specifically, Benson's efforts to do away with government price supports.[18] In a spirited sermon presented to church faithful in March 1953, Lee proclaimed: "There will be many who will belittle him [Elder Benson] and will try to destroy his reputation and destroy his influence in high places. But I want to say to you that those who do will be forgotten in the remains of Mother Earth, and the odor of their infamy will ever be with them. Whereas glory and majesty will be attached to the name of Ezra Taft Benson."[19]

*

Given the changes within the Twelve in just three years, Lee found himself second in seniority. Only the venerable Joseph Fielding Smith ranked ahead of him. Not surprisingly, Lee played an ever more dominant role in quorum deliberations. Lee also continued his hectic schedule of travel to officiate over stake conferences

---

16. Gibbons, 299.

17. As quoted by Lee, in Gibbons, 299.

18. As quoted by Lee, in Gibbons, 302.

19. Remarks by Elder Harold B. Lee to Washington, DC Stake conference, Mar. 1, 1953, typescript, box 84, fd. 14, MS 164, in J. Willard Marriott Papers, Special Collections, J. Willard Marriott Library, University of Utah.

throughout Utah and beyond. In fact, his schedule expanded to include travel to centers of church activity outside the United States.

The church experienced unprecedented growth during this period. Total membership surged from 1,147,000 in 1951 to 1,823,000 by 1961—an increase of 570,000, or 50 percent. The annual rate of growth accelerated from 3.5 percent to 5.9 percent.

In November 1951 Lee was given yet another assignment, appointment to the church Board of Education's executive committee. Chaired by quorum president Joseph Fielding Smith, the board's other members included Apostles Henry D. Moyle and Marion G. Romney. Its responsibilities involved overseeing the church's extensive education system, which included BYU, Ricks College (Idaho), and the Church College at Hawaii, along with all seminaries and institutes. Lee joined the board at a time when BYU was beginning to undergo significant expansion of its physical plant along with upgrading of the professional standing of its faculty. Promoting all such expansion was Ernest L. Wilkinson—BYU's newly appointed, dynamic fifty-year-old president. Over the following years, Lee and Wilkinson worked together, albeit not always amicably.[20]

Meanwhile, Lee continued as managing director of the Church Welfare Program. By the 1950s, however, the entire program was coming under increased scrutiny, causing McKay to reevaluate how it was being administered. On the local level, there "was concern about the heavy, continuing welfare assessments imposed by the General Welfare Committee." Some LDS businessmen "protested against the sale of welfare commodities in the open market in direct competition." Certain church leaders, moreover, felt "there had been an undue proliferation of welfare projects beyond what was strictly necessary."[21]

In fact, the situation of high unemployment and economic depression that had spawned the program's development no longer existed, given the prosperity of the 1950s. Accordingly, McKay approved "some trimming" along with a "reining in of its growth." All of this caused anxiety for Lee concerning the future of the program. In response, he took a "cautious approach to any proposal to expand it," concerned that such an attempt "might precipitate further

20. Gibbons, 294.

21. Such observations were stated by Francis M. Gibbons himself, Gibbons, 294–95.

cutbacks." Ultimately McKay affirmed support for the program as a whole, declaring that "its methods ... tested and proved sound" while also extolling Lee's leadership.[22] Relieved, Lee frankly told the church president that he felt "as though the welfare program had been gained a reprieve."[23]

In August 1953, Lee was appointed to the temple committee, chaired by Joseph Fielding Smith, president of the Quorum of the Twelve. Lee's responsibilities involved general supervision over all temples, including arranging solemn assemblies and other temple activities. He arranged the cornerstone-laying ceremonies for the Los Angeles temple and took charge of its dedication in March 1956.[24]

*

During the seven years from 1954 through 1961, Lee undertook five major trips abroad on behalf of the church.

The apostle's first major trip, in late 1954, took him to the Far East. Lee carried out two responsibilities during the course of his 20,000-mile, six-nation journey. First, as chair of the LDS Servicemen's Committee, he visited and assessed the condition of some 1,500 LDS military personnel stationed at bases throughout the area. Second, he evaluated church missionary efforts and visited both missionaries and local church leaders.

Lee departed the United States in early August 1954, accompanied by his wife, Fern. Travelling by ship, the Lees were joined by BYU president Ernest L. Wilkinson, traveling as far as Hawaii to assess the prospects of establishing a church-sponsored junior college there. The two men discussed this item along with other matters of church education.[25]

Following a brief stopover in Hawaii, the Lees continued to Yokohama, Japan. Lee first met with Japan mission president Hilton A. Robertson and visited with some 200 church members gathered for church services. Next, he moved on to the nearby 8th Army Base to visit LDS servicemen. He was "outfitted with army clothing and insignia enabling him to visit army camps as a VIP with all the

22. Gibbons, 296–97.
23. As recalled by Lee, in Gibbons, 297.
24. Gibbons, 308–309.
25. Gibbons, 316–17.

privileges normally accorded a major general."[26] Moving on from Yokohama, the Lees visited local LDS congregations in Sapporo, Tokyo, Itazuki, and Osaka.[27]

Leaving Japan, the visitors moved on to South Korea—still recovering from the ravages of the recently concluded Korean Conflict. In Seoul, Lee toured a US Army base and presided over a local conference of LDS servicemen along with a few Korean converts. The Lees next visited Pusan where they met with LDS servicemen and local church members. Among the most memorable activities was flying over the demilitarized zone (DMZ), the site of the recent, bitter fighting between the two sides. When one of the commanding generals heard Lee's last name, he remarked, "Well, you have a lot of relatives in this country," adding that "the five most prominent names in Korea are Yi, Chang, Kim, Pak, and Lee."[28]

Returning to Tokyo, the Lees attended yet more meetings, including with LDS missionaries. Following visits to two other Japanese cities, Sendai and Nikko, they moved on to Okinawa—site of the bloodiest fighting in the Pacific during World War II. The Lees then traveled to Taiwan and Hong Kong to meet with local Latter-day Saints, and then continued to the Philippines where he met with LDS servicemen at Clark Field. The journey concluded with brief stops at Guam and Wake Island.[29]

Lee's eight-week tour of the Far East was significant in that he became convinced that the region held great potential for future church growth. He informed McKay of this fact and called for the acceleration of missionary activity in the region. His personal, up-close interactions with Asians convinced him that they would make ideal converts.[30]

Some two years later, in June 1956, Lee ventured once more abroad, this time to Mexico, accompanied by Spencer W. Kimball. They started out by train from Salt Lake City to El Paso, and then took an automobile to Mexico City. The main purpose of the trip was to set apart a new mission president, Joseph T. Bentley. Upon

---

26. Gibbons, 318.
27. Gibbons, 319.
28. As recalled by Lee, in Goates, 246.
29. Gibbons, 322–24.
30. Gibbons, 325.

the apostles' arrival, Bentley introduced them to Rex E. Lee—a young missionary whom Bentley asked to be set apart as his second counselor.[31] Rex Lee, no relation to Harold Lee, was a direct descendent of notorious southern Utah pioneer John D. Lee.[32] Rex Lee would go on to become US Solicitor General and later president of Brigham Young University.

Lee and Kimball traveled next to Cuernavaca and Vera Cruz where they met with church members. They also visited the historic Yucatan peninsula where, according to popular Mormon folklore, "the Land Bountiful" of the Book of Mormon was located and "near the alleged center where the Savior made his appearance to the Nephites." In that same spot, Lee claimed to have "found evidences of Christianity followed by pagan or mystic corruptions which all but obliterated the simple Christian doctrines or Mosaic observances which were probably practiced here."[33] Following that, the two apostles returned to Utah.

Lee's third trip abroad, in October 1958, took him to South Africa. His assignment involved assessing LDS progress in that country since McKay's own visit some four year earlier. In the wake of McKay's 1954 visit, the church had eased somewhat on its policy requiring that any LDS male seeking priesthood ordination provide genealogical evidence that he had no black African ancestry. After 1954, any LDS male who did not physically exhibit black African ancestry could be ordained to the priesthood. (The racist LDS policy regarding blacks and the priesthood and temple participation was abandoned in 1978.) South African church membership more than doubled during this period, from 1,372 in 1950 to 2,901 by 1960.[34]

Despite this, as Lee discovered, South African Latter-day Saints continued to grapple with race—exacerbated by the apartheid policies imposed by that nation's white minority on its black majority. Blacks were "becoming more and more vocal and sometimes violent

---

31. Goates, 260–61; Gibbons, 332–33.

32. A good biography of John D. Lee is Juanita Brooks, *John Doyle Lee: Zealot, Pioneer, Builder, Scapegoat* (Glendale, California: Arthur H. Clark Co., 1961).

33. As noted by Goates, 263.

34. For a discussion of this development, see Newell G. Bringhurst, "David O. McKay's Confrontation with Mormonism's Black Priesthood Ban," *John Whitmer Historical Association Journal* 37, no. 2 (Fall/Winter 2017): 1–11.

in their opposition to Apartheid."[35] Church members in Durban expressed fears that the black population, which far outnumbered whites, would one day unite under Communism to take control of the country. Alarmed church members discussed with Lee the possibility of emigrating, *en masse*, to the United States and/or Canada.[36]

Lee confronted a different racial problem upon visiting Port Elizabeth where he presided over the dedication of a new church meetinghouse. He was approached by three young Latter-day Saint women with "mixed blood" who asked him "what the Lord would have them do about marriage and having children." After giving the three members priesthood blessings, Lee wrote in his journal, "The Spirit seemed to indicate that they [the young women] should seek for a husband who likewise has mixed blood." He further added, "I gave them assurances of their eternal blessings if they would live up to all they are permitted to do in their present state." The visiting apostle, in fact, talked with "many members of mixed blood who came to discuss this problem" with him.[37] Thus, Lee returned to the United States with a greater awareness of the consequences of Mormonism's racist policy.

Lee's fourth, and most extensive, journey took him to Latin America in late 1959. His assignment was to organize two new missions, one in Brazil and one in the Andes region of Chile and Peru. Lee, again accompanied by Fern, left the United States on August 29, 1959, embarking on a three-month odyssey. The Lees were joined by Asael Sorenson—called as president of the new Brazil South Mission.[38] By this time total church membership in Brazil numbered some 2,600—a three-fold increase over the 650 a decade earlier.

Brazilian missionary efforts were concentrated in southern Brazil since the region had a lower percentage of mixed-race Brazilians. Rulon S. Howells, the previous Brazil Mission president, had established a policy of avoiding Brazilians of known African ancestry. Also established under Howell's leadership was the requirement, identical to the policy in South Africa, that any Brazilian male

---

35. Gibbons, 364.
36. Goates, 266.
37. As stated by Lee, in Goates, 269.
38. Goates, 280; Gibbons, 374–76.

member desiring priesthood ordination provide genealogical proof that he possessed no African ancestry.[39]

Despite such restrictions, a handful of black Brazilians joined the church—as Lee discovered during his visit to Bauru, a municipality in Sao Paulo, where he found a number of black members. Lee described in his journal the following: "a black woman president of the branch Relief Society with her husband and children all members, and a young girl with black blood in charge of the Primary. Both tell me, [they] are well received by the whites."[40]

From Brazil, the Lees traveled to Uruguay, spending time in Montevideo to preside over a conference of six hundred local Saints.[41] From there, the visitors moved on to Paraguay, where Lee presided over a conference at Isla Petrulla. In Argentina Lee found the largest number of church members, numbering 3,500—a threefold increase from that of a decade earlier. In Buenos Aires, Lee presided over a church conference of six hundred members before moving on to Chile.[42]

Following his arrival in Santiago, Chile, Lee presided over the organization of the new Andes Mission, whose jurisdiction covered the nations of Chile and Peru. At the time of its formation, the Andes Mission consisted of eight hundred members in twelve branches in both countries. Lima, Peru, served as the headquarters of the mission, with Vernon Sharp as its president.[43]

Lee and Fern then traveled northward to Central America where they met church members in Costa Rica and El Salvador. Next came Guatemala where Lee reported to have enjoyed "some of the greatest spiritual experiences of the entire trip." "Most thrilling" was Lee's interaction with some 1,600 members whom he characterized as "among the most distinctive Lamanite people I have yet been among. Sometimes I had a strong feeling that this place is without question the Lamanite capital of North America and that a temple

---

39. Mark L. Grover, "Religious Accommodation in the Land of Democracy: Mormon Priesthood and Black Brazilians," *Dialogue: A Journal of Mormon Thought* 17, no. 3 (Autumn 1984): 23–34.

40. Lee's diary, as recorded in Goates, 280–81.

41. As recorded by Lee, in Goates, 283.

42. Goates, 284–85.

43. Goates, 285–90.

for the Latin American people should be built here."[44] After a final stop in Mexico City, where the apostle met local church members,[45] the Lees returned to Salt Lake City in mid-November.

A mere three months later, in March 1960, the much-traveled Lee embarked on yet another international journey—to Great Britain. Lee's assignment was to organize the church's first British stake, located in Manchester, England. The stake, composed of nine wards and two branches, accommodated 2,400 church members. During the same visit, Lee presided over the division of the British Mission, creating the North British Mission, headquartered in Liverpool. These actions set the stage for a period of rapid growth throughout the British Isles over the following decade.[46]

Taken together, all five of Lee's trips provided the apostle with a keen awareness of the diverse, distinctive peoples whom he encountered and made him more sensitive to their needs. He was able to bear witness to the evolution of the LDS Church into a truly international organization.

*

When not traveling abroad, Lee continued his array of routine duties such as presiding over stake conferences in Utah and out of state as well as presiding over an ever-increasing number of temple marriage ceremonies.

The busy apostle also spent a considerable portion of this time preparing and delivering sermons and inspirational talks to church faithful on a range of topics and in a variety of venues, the most important being the church's semi-annual general conferences. Such presentations further enhanced his reputation as a dynamic speaker and proponent of conservative church doctrine.

Two general conference sermons are particularly noteworthy. The first, "Blessed Is He That Cometh in the Name of the Lord," was presented in April 1955 to mark the commemoration of Easter. It was broadcast on "Church of the Air" to a nationwide audience, and

---

44. As quoted from Lee's diary, in Goates, 290–91.
45. Goates, 293.
46. Goates, 294–99.

thus enjoyed a favorable response from both within and outside of the LDS community.[47]

Lee's second major sermon was presented at the October 1956 general conference and was entitled "The Preparation of the People for the Beginning of the Millennial Reign." Lee gave his sobering address at a very anxious time in American history, given increased Cold War tensions between the United States and the Soviet Union. Both nations developed nuclear weapons capable of destroying each other, and many were asking: "Are the end times near?" While avoiding answering the question directly, Lee "acknowledged the reality of it and the need for the wise to be prepared."[48]

*

By the mid-1950s, Lee had gained a well-earned reputation as an effective, dynamic leader who was able to get things done, which, in turn, led to invitations to join the boards of directors of a number of non-Mormon corporations.

Among the most important was the Union Pacific Railroad, whose corporate board he joined in November 1956. At the time, the Union Pacific was among the most powerful enterprises in the nation. Company officials saw Lee as hard-working, creative, and persistent. Lee, moreover, possessed broad business acumen by virtue of his membership on the boards of directors of a number of LDS Church-owned companies. Lee viewed membership on the Union Pacific board as an opportunity to exert "influence in temporal affairs far beyond the influence of the LDS Church."[49] (Membership on such national boards also helped to supplement the income of the church's full-time clergy.)

Some two years later, in June 1958, Lee accepted an invitation to join the board of directors of the Equitable Life Insurance Company, based in New York. In joining the Equitable Life board, Lee filled a vacancy created by the retirement of J. Reuben Clark. Clark, in fact, urged the appointment of his protégé. Membership on the Equitable board brought Lee into contact with, according to one of his biographers, "some of America's most able and influential

---

47. Gibbons, 325–26.
48. Gibbons, 335.
49. Gibbons, 337–40.

business and professional leaders." Lee's association with these men, in turn, "opened a new window of understanding ... broadening his perceptions of society in general, increasing his knowledge of management strategies and skills, and enlarging his network of influence, both personally and for the Church."[50]

*

Meanwhile, during the late 1950s, the church experienced significant leadership changes with the passing of a number of general authorities.

In February 1958, Adam S. Bennion passed away at age seventy-one, having served just five years as an apostle. This paved the way for Hugh B. Brown, who was ordained an apostle that April. Brown had served as an assistant to the Twelve the previous five years and, prior to that, had compiled a long record of church service in a variety of callings. Lee, whom Brown knew well and had worked closely with over the years, expressed pleasure at the seventy-five-year old's overdue elevation to the Twelve. Brown had "been prominently mentioned for appointment to fill a vacancy in the Quorum of the Twelve" as early as April 1941.[51]

First Presidency counselor Stephen L. Richards's death in May 1959 created yet another vacancy. McKay had looked upon Richards as both a valued advisor and close friend. McKay was so devastated by Richards's death that he delayed naming a replacement,[52] but ultimately named J. Reuben Clark as first counselor. The six senior members of the Twelve were Clark protégés and/or embraced his philosophy.[53] McKay called Apostle Henry D. Moyle to replace Clark as second counselor. Lee expressed extreme pleasure with both appointments, remarking, "It seemed to me almost too good to be true."[54]

Lee had enjoyed his association with both Clark and Moyle over the previous two decades and looked forward to working with both men. Concerning Moyle, with whom he had sometimes butted heads in the past, Lee, stated: "It is becoming increasingly clear that

---

50. Gibbons, 357–58.

51. Lee, as quoted in Goates, 165; Gibbons, 187.

52. As quoted in Quinn, *Elder Statesman*, 179.

53. As noted in Quinn, *Elder Statesman*, 170.

54. As Lee recorded in his diary for the date June 12, 1959, and noted in Gibbons, 257, and Goates, 335.

Brother Moyle is going to be an aggressive mover of plans representing the First Presidency."[55]

Filling Moyle's vacancy in the Twelve was Howard W. Hunter, called in October 1959. Hunter, like Lee, was an Idaho native, born and raised in Boise. As a young man in his early twenties, he moved to California where he attended law school and subsequently built up a successful law practice. As an effective, innovative president of the Pasadena Stake from 1950 to 1959, Hunter implemented seminary education for local students, reformed the stake's welfare plan, and introduced Family Home Evening on the stake level—the latter program ultimately implemented on a churchwide basis.[56]

Clark's two-year tenure as McKay's first counselor, from 1959 to 1961, proved less than ideal as he found himself isolated from essential decision making. Lee noted that his mentor brooded "over matters about which he is not kept too well informed," while another Clark protégé, Apostle Marion G. Romney, observed, "He feels like he's unwanted and useless."[57]

Clark's situation was made worse by the steady deterioration of his health. He suffered from a series of progressively debilitating maladies, beginning with frequent colds and flu, advancing to coronary problems, and followed by Bell's palsy. Added to this was a loss of mobility, requiring his use of a wheelchair.[58]

By June 1961, Clark was so frustrated by his situation that he asked McKay to release him, proclaiming, "Idleness is not happiness." Such a move would have been unprecedented, and McKay refused. Instead, McKay appointed Hugh B. Brown as a "special counselor" in the First Presidency. Aware of the implications, Clark reacted emotionally. He "wept like the dickens," recalled Lee.[59] Thus, Clark "was functionally, though not officially replaced in the First Presidency."[60]

Clark lingered for another four months before dying at home on

55. As recorded by Lee in his diary for July 14, 1959, and noted by Goates, 336.

56. For an overview of Howard W. Hunter's life, see Eleanor Knowles, *Howard W. Hunter* (Salt Lake City: Deseret Book Co., 1994).

57. Both Lee and Romney's observations as quoted in Quinn, *Elder Statesman*, 174–75.

58. Quinn, *Elder Statesman*, 176.

59. As recalled in Lee's diary, June 22, 1961, as quoted in Quinn, *Elder Statesman*, 177.

60. Quinn, *Elder Statesman*, 177.

October 6, 1961. At Clark's funeral service, Lee, in a heartfelt eulogy, proclaimed his mentor "the most influential man in his life."[61] On a later occasion Lee described their relationship in these terms: "No father was ever closer to a son than President Clark has been to me."[62]

Clark's demise necessitated further leadership changes. In October 1961, Gordon B. Hinckley was called to the Quorum of the Twelve to fill the vacancy created by the elevation of Brown to the First Presidency. Hinckley, fifty-one years old at the time, was born and raised in Salt Lake City. He graduated from the University of Utah with a BA in English literature, and was drawn to journalism and media publicity, in which capacity he served the church over the following decades. He assumed a prominent role on the church's Radio, Publicity, and Missionary Literature Committee commencing in the 1930s. He also served on the church Sunday school board and on the board of directors for KSL—the church-owned radio and television station. In 1958 he was called as an assistant to the Twelve and assumed primary responsibility for LDS activity in the Far East. Hinckley was involved in the development of the church's first standardized missionary lesson plan.[63]

During the 1950s the Quorum of the Twelve went through an almost complete transformation relative to membership, with eight new apostles. Six of the Twelve were destined to lead the church through the twentieth century and into the twenty-first: Joseph Fielding Smith, Harold B. Lee, Spencer W. Kimball, Ezra Taft Benson, Howard W. Hunter, and Gordon B. Hinckley—this reflective of a decline in the average age of the members of the Twelve.

Another important change in church leadership involved an increase in the number of assistants to the Twelve along with the expansion of their assigned duties. When the office was created in 1941 just five men were appointed to the office, a number that did not increase over the next ten years. During the 1950s, McKay increased the number of assistants to fifteen. During this same decade,

---

61. Goates, 342.

62. William Grant Bangerter, as quoted in Goates, 288.

63. The authorized biography of Gordon B. Hinkley is Sheri L. Dew, *Go Forward with Faith: The Biography of Gordon B. Hinckley* (Salt Lake City: Deseret Book Co., 1996); also see Gary James Bergera, "Gordon B. Hinckley," in Ardis Parshall and W. Paul Reeve, eds., *Mormonism: A Historical Encyclopedia* (Santa Barbara: ABC-CLIO, 2010).

the duties of the assistants also significantly expanded. By 1960, assistants were required to preside over and speak at stake conferences, reorganize stakes, and facilitate missionary work at home and abroad. This change helped to ease the increasing burden borne by the Twelve and the First Presidency.[64]

*

Lee insisted on being continually engaged in useful, productive activity—preferably in the service of the church, the primary focus of his existence. Indeed, he found all forms of idleness distasteful. "The hardest work I do, I have discovered, is to loaf for a few days with nothing to do."[65]

However, the ever-busy apostle found that gardening provided a welcome respite from his never-ending church responsibilities. Tending the yard and garden at his westside Salt Lake City home provided relaxation and a sense of accomplishment. When the Lees moved to an apartment in downtown Salt Lake City in 1949, he soon found he sorely missed gardening. Thus, in October 1951, the Lees purchased a 2,400-square-foot two-story home that included a spacious yard at 849 Connor Street on the city's east bench. Having a yard to putter in again enabled Lee "to work off his frustrations."[66]

Some ten years later, the Lees were compelled to move due to Fern's deteriorating health. A major consideration in their 1961 purchase of an even more upscale home at 1436 Penrose Drive in Salt Lake City's tony Federal Heights neighborhood was the rambler's ability to accommodate Fern with her chronic heart condition and increasingly frail health.[67]

Meanwhile, Lee suffered from ongoing health problems of his own. In March 1953 he complained of "considerable distress" in his "abdominal region" along with "recurring headaches."[68] He also suffered from recurring sinus problems. The latter problem was eventually corrected through surgery performed April 1954. For several years thereafter, Lee was free of any major physical problems

---

64. Gibbons, 386–87.
65. As quoted in Goates, 274.
66. Gibbons, 290–91.
67. Goates, 342–43.
68. Gibbons, 303.

with the exception of what he referred to as a bout of "nervous tension" in late 1955.[69]

By 1958, however, Lee faced a new series of health problems. In July of that year, he was rushed to the LDS Hospital with "internal hemorrhaging" caused by a "bleeding ulcer in the duodenal canal." This condition, detected a year earlier, had been left untreated. The ailing apostle was placed on a strict diet and ordered to rest, which, not surprisingly, he found difficult to do.[70] Indeed, a year earlier he had lamented in his diary, "It was my fifty-eighth birthday with the realization that advancing years bring increased problems and anxieties."[71]

The death of Lee's mother that same July added to the strain of recovering from his bleeding ulcer. Louisa Bingham Lee was eighty years old at the time of her death from a heart attack. Lee summarized her life thus: "Everything seemed to be in perfect harmony with mother's life, whose last days were, as the patriarch promised years ago, 'her best days.' She was ready to go home. She had saved the entire cost of her burial and last illness."[72]

*

In June 1959 Lee was compelled to give up his longtime position as managing director of the Church Welfare Program. Prompting his release was the increasing number of his other responsibilities.[73]

As he looked toward completing his second decade as a general authority, he anticipated undertaking an even more daunting task, implementing the long-delayed but carefully crafted plans for correlation, which he deemed especially urgent given the church's growth in membership and geographic expansion.

---

69. Gibbons, 315.
70. Goates, 279; Goates, 358–59.
71. Gibbons, 343.
72. Lee, as quoted in Goates, 278.
73. Gibbons, 389.

CHAPTER SEVEN

AN EXPANDING CHURCH
1961-70

The 1960s are remembered primarily as a period of political and social upheaval. Most noteworthy were the assassinations of John F. Kennedy (1963), Martin Luther King Jr. (1968), and Robert F. Kennedy (1968); the racial unrest culminating in rioting in dozens of American cities; and the seemingly never-ending Vietnam War. All such events brought about profound changes that affected American society in ways that continue to be felt today.

Concurrently, the LDS Church experienced major changes and encountered controversies of its own as it continued to expand at a record rate both within the United States and abroad.

By far the most important of these changes was the Correlation Program which Lee promoted with his well-honed qualities of drive, determination, and tenacity. But Lee and his fellow general authorities were compelled to confront other issues as well, including budgetary problems that developed into a full-scale crisis during the early 1960s. Also, the church in general and Lee in particular confronted the increasingly controversial issue of race and the subordinate status of black people. On a personal level, Lee dealt with tragedy in his immediate family and with his own chronic health problems.

*

The First Presidency and Quorum of the Twelve experienced a significant shift in composition, foreshadowing important changes within the church itself.

Two new apostles were called to the Twelve: N. Eldon Tanner and Thomas S. Monson, both of whom enjoyed a working relationship with Lee.

Tanner was ordained an apostle in October 1962, replacing the eighty-eight-year-old George Q. Morris, who died the previous April. Sixty-four-year-old Tanner, a distant cousin of Fern Tanner Lee, was born in Salt Lake City but came of age in Cardston, Alberta, Canada. After graduating from Calgary Normal School, Tanner taught high school and subsequently distinguished himself in Provincial politics as a member of the Social Credit Party. He served in the Alberta Legislative Assembly and as Provincial Minister of Lands and Mines. Tanner married Sara Isabelle Merrill, and together they had five daughters. In the church, he was president of the Calgary Alberta Stake—a calling championed by Lee and Hugh B. Brown, Tanner's uncle. In 1960, Tanner was named an assistant to the Twelve.

Tanner's rise in the church hierarchy proved meteoric as, just two years later, in October 1962, he joined the Twelve. The following year he replaced Henry D. Moyle as second counselor to David O. McKay. (Moyle had died unexpectedly in September 1963 in Florida.) Tanner's appointment surprised many, as he was the most junior member of the Twelve.[1]

Replacing Tanner in the Twelve was Thomas S. Monson. Thirty-six years old at the time of his ordination, Monson was born and grew up on the west side of Salt Lake City. As a member of the Pioneer Stake, he developed a close relationship with then-stake president Harold B. Lee. After completing high school, Monson graduated from the University of Utah. He went into a career in printing and advertising, initially with the *Deseret News* as an advertising executive, and then with the Deseret News Press as general manager. He married Frances Beverly Johnson; they had three children.

Through his various church callings, Monson manifested an inherent, deeply felt empathy for other people, especially those in grief. At age twenty-two he was called as a bishop—ordained by Lee—and drew close to the ward's large, 1,000-member congregation, paying particular attention to the needs of its fifty-five widows. He was called as president of the Canadian Mission at thirty-one and succeeded in building it up, increasing the number of converts, and

---

1. Gibbons, 311–12.

expanding the scope of its operations. Monson's subsequent elevation to the Twelve made him the youngest apostle in fifty-three years.
Meanwhile, Lee continued to mentor his young, capable protégé.[2]

In addition to Monson, Lee took two other promising church
leaders under his wing: Alvin R. Dyer and Boyd K. Packer.

Dyer, born and raised in Salt Lake City, built up and managed a
successful heating and air conditioning business. He married May
Elizabeth Jackson and they became the parents of two children. His
church service included a calling as bishop of the Monument Park
Ward. Lee, as a member of the ward, became well-acquainted with
the energetic bishop. Dyer was subsequently called as president of
the Central States Mission in 1954. Upon visiting the mission and
assessing Dyer's success, Lee proclaimed him "a master craftsman of
human engineering."[3] Dyer was called as an assistant to the Twelve
in 1958. With this calling came Dyer's appointment as president of
the European Mission during the early 1960s.[4]

Packer, another Lee protégé, was born and raised in Brigham
City, Utah. Coming of age during World War II, he served as a
bomber pilot in the Army Air Force. Upon his return to civilian
life, he attended Weber State College, Utah State University, and
Brigham Young University where he earned an EdD. He served the
church as a professional educator, ultimately overseeing the church's
network of seminaries and institutes of religion. He married Donna
Smith in 1947; they became the parents of ten children.

Packer and Lee came to know each other through their work
together on the church Board of Education executive committee. In
an August 1957 meeting, Lee informed Packer of his dissatisfaction
with the way the seminary and institute program was being run,
noting certain staff and teachers who he claimed manifested "un-
orthodox views on doctrine and on the mission of the Church" and
insisting that such individuals were "creating confusion and in some
instances, apostasy among the students." Lee encouraged Packer to
undertake corrective measures, which Packer did. As a result, Packer

---

2. Gibbons, 335–36. For an overview of Monson's life, see Heidi R. Swinton, *To
the Rescue: The Biography of Thomas S. Monson* (Salt Lake City: Deseret Book Co., 2010).

3. Lee, as quoted in Gibbons, 327.

4. Goates, 294.

became a Lee protégé and was subsequently appointed to the church Council for Seminaries and Institutes. Working together, the two men exerted "a strong influence on the policies governing church schools, altering the deficiencies in the administration of seminaries and institutes."[5] This, in turn, earned the thirty-six-year-old Packer a call to serve as an assistant to the Twelve in 1961.

In October 1965 McKay called two additional counselors to the First Presidency, president of the Twelve Joseph Fielding Smith and assistant to the Twelve Thorpe B. Isaacson. Smith and Isaacson joined counselors Brown and Tanner, thereby increasing to four the number of First Presidency counselors. Concurrently, Smith remained president of the Twelve. Thus, Lee, second to Smith in seniority, assumed a number of Smith's quorum-related responsibilities.

Meanwhile, Isaacson suffered a massive stroke just three months after assuming office. This compelled McKay to select yet another First Presidency counselor. McKay called Dyer, who, like Isaacson, had previously served as an assistant to the Twelve.[6] Dyer's appointment was problematic in that McKay had not consulted either Brown or Tanner beforehand.[7]

*

Lee's main focus throughout this period was on implementing his long-sought plans for churchwide correlation.

The first step involved consolidating the teaching of church curriculum. Up to this time the various church auxiliaries—specifically the Relief Society, Sunday schools, Primary, MIA, and priesthood quorums—had acted independently to prepare instructional materials. Working through the General Priesthood Committee, Lee pushed through a series of measures to consolidate and systematize the various teaching materials used by these auxiliary and priesthood organizations.[8]

Following that, Lee promoted a long-range, comprehensive plan of priesthood-directed correlation, developed in consultation with

---

5. Lee, as quoted in Gibbons, 348–49.

6. Gibbons, 411–12.

7. For a discussion of this unusual episode involving McKay's First Presidency, see Gary James Bergera, "Tensions in David O. McKay's First Presidencies," *Journal of Mormon History* 33, no. 1 (Spring 2007), 179–246.

8. Gibbons, 389; Goates, 366.

a specially appointed All Church Coordinating Council. The General Priesthood Board was created and subsequently divided into four priesthood components—each assuming a specific area of responsibility and each under the supervision of a general authority. The four components were (1) missionary, chaired by president Joseph Fielding Smith; (2) priesthood—later designated the home teaching committee—chaired by Apostle Marion G. Romney; (3) genealogical, under the direction of Apostle N. Eldon Tanner; and (4) welfare, chaired by Presiding Bishop John H. Vandenburg. Also established were three additional correlation committees, each focusing on the church's three major age groups and each chaired by a member of the Twelve. Romney chaired the adult member committee; Richard L. Evans, the committee on youth; and Gordon B. Hinckley, children. Together, all seven committees oversaw the ongoing process of correlation.[9]

In pushing the correlation process forward, Lee authorized the creation of a new level of leadership within church bureaucracy: regional representative. Within the church hierarchy, regional representatives occupied a position below the Quorum of the Twelve and above stake presidents. These new officials represented the Twelve in overseeing the training of local leaders. In essence a staff position, regional representatives served without compensation for a period of years.[10]

The correlation program itself was implemented gradually during the 1960s and into the 1970s. On the ward level, correlation mandated changes in the ward teaching program, which was renamed "home teaching" and placed under the supervision of priesthood quorum leaders. Priesthood holders doing home teaching were instructed to do more than simply make their traditional monthly visits to members' homes. They were to become personally acquainted with all family members. Correlation further mandated that each ward organize a ward council made up of its priesthood executive committee and the heads of all the auxiliaries to coordinate ward functions and deal with other matters. Also launched on the ward level in 1965 was the Family Home Evening program, wherein families were advised to spend at least one night together in some form

9. Gibbons, 390–91.
10. Gibbons, 413–14; Goates, 374–75.

of interactive recreational/educational/spiritual activity. Specially prepared manuals provided suggested lessons and activities.[11] Such reforms were implemented with little difficulty.

More controversial were efforts by Lee and associates to implement sweeping correlation measures mandating the reining in of churchwide auxiliary organizations—specifically, the Relief Society, Mutual Improvement Association (MIA), Primary, and Sunday school. Not surprisingly, the auxiliaries resisted such changes.[12] Their leaders, in the words of one observer, "did not want to relinquish their control. They had huge general boards. They had all the talent in the Church marshaled at their command. They had [their own] budgets."[13] Thus, much to Lee's chagrin, the long-standing and deeply entrenched bureaucracies of the auxiliary organizations managed to forestall the more sweeping reforms. Such was the case with the Relief Society, the most powerful of the auxiliaries and headed by the formidable Belle Smith Spafford.[14]

Ultimately, Lee succeeded in pushing through the major elements of correlation, specifically coordinating the functions of all church organizations and transferring the budgets of the auxiliaries to the General Church Operating Fund. Also involved was termination of the publications issued by each of the auxiliaries. Issued in their place were three age-grouped magazines—the *Ensign*, the *New Era*, and the *Friend*. In essence, all church organizations were brought under direct priesthood control.[15]

*

Lee and his fellow general authorities were also forced to deal with a more pressing, indeed critical, problem: an acute budget crisis that beset the church during the early 1960s. Specifically, church expenses exceeded revenue, with annual deficits running into the millions of dollars.

---

11. James B. Allen and Glen M. Leonard, *The Story of the Latter-day Saints*, 2nd ed. (Salt Lake City: Deseret Book Co., 1992), 596–99.

12. Gregory A. Prince and Wm Robert Wright, *David O. McKay and the Rise of Modern Mormonism* (Salt Lake City: University of Utah Press, 2005), 155–58.

13. As noted in May 20, 1996, interview of Brent Goates by Gregory Prince, as quoted in Prince and Wright, *David O. McKay,* 155.

14. Prince and Wright, *David O. McKay,* 157.

15. Prince and Wright, *David O. McKay,* 157–58.

The underlying cause of the budget crisis was the church's ambitious building program commenced during the late 1950s and continuing into the early 1960s. By the end of 1960, the church had 800 church buildings worldwide under construction. Some 1,941 (55 percent) of the total 3,500 LDS meetinghouses worldwide had been built since 1951.[16] The driving force behind this massive building program was First Presidency counselor Henry D. Moyle and Wendell B. Mendenhall, chair of the Church Building Committee.[17] Through the construction of attractive, modern meetinghouses, Moyle and Mendenhall sought to grow the church, particularly in those countries where it had struggled. At the same time, Moyle and Mendenhall wanted to improve the church's image and thereby attract increasing numbers of new converts. In this regard, the program succeeded. During each of the five years from 1961 through 1965, the church boasted the five highest annual numbers of convert baptisms in its history.[18]

But at the same time, church spending exceeded revenues, causing concern among fiscally conservative leaders. In particular, Lee, given his role on the Church Expenditure Committee, expressed his "stubborn resistance to the principle of deficit spending" in any way, shape, or form.[19] Moyle countered Lee, asserting that he "did not view the funding of new chapels as deficit spending," further characterizing it "an excellent investment. New chapels would result in new converts who, in turn, would provide new sources of tithing revenue that would service the debt."[20] Unconvinced, Lee continued his outspoken opposition, affirming, "There is still some cloudiness as to where the money is to come from to finance" all such expenditures. Lee then went on to ridicule deficit spending as "a philosophy of spending ourselves into prosperity."[21] As the deficits continued to mount, Lee gained support from fellow members of the Church Expenditure Committee as well as other general authorities.[22] In

---

16. Prince and Wright, *David O. McKay*, 208–209.
17. As quoted in the Church News section of *Deseret News*, July 23, 1960.
18. Prince and Wright, *David O. McKay*, 209.
19. Lee, as quoted in Goates, 381.
20. Moyle, as quoted in Prince and Wright, *David O. McKay*, 210.
21. Lee, as quoted in Goates, 384.
22. Goates, 381.

the midst of this controversy, Moyle died unexpectedly of a massive heart attack in September 1963.[23]

N. Eldon Tanner, who replaced Moyle in the First Presidency, took a different position. Tanner, whom Lee knew and trusted, possessed "keen business instincts ... outstanding personal skills" and most important "an intense desire to bring church finances back under control."[24] Upon assuming his position as second counselor in October 1963, Tanner implemented a number of changes, specifically, purchasing and accounting reforms along with delays in new projects to ease cash-flow problems.[25] In pushing forward with further reforms, Tanner accepted the resignation of Mendenhall as chair of the building committee in 1965.[26] With both Mendenhall and Moyle gone, church spending was brought back into line with revenue.

*

Lee found himself confronted with another pressing issue: the church's increasingly controversial black priesthood and temple ban, which was coming under intense scrutiny both within and outside of the LDS community.

Throughout the years of his apostolic ministry, Lee repeatedly made clear his conviction that the ban was divinely sanctioned. Lee's earliest statement of support was his "Youth of a Noble Birthright" sermon, delivered as a radio speech in May 1945 and published first as an article in the *Deseret News*, then as a church-authorized pamphlet, and ultimately as a chapter in his first book, *Youth and the Church*.[27] Lee's basic arguments justifying the ban—the alleged misbehavior of black people in the pre-existence along with the assertion that their dark skin was emblematic of their status as the accursed descendants of Cain—echoed the previously stated views of other church officials.[28]

---

23. Prince and Wright, *David O. McKay*, 215.

24. As quoted in Prince and Wright, *David O. McKay*, 215.

25. Prince and Wright, *David O. McKay*, 215–16.

26. Prince and Wright, *David O. McKay*, 221.

27. Lee, "Youth of a Noble Birthright," address delivered Sunday, May 6, 1945, over KSL Radio; Lee, "Youth of a Noble Birthright," Church News section of *Deseret News*, May 12, 1945; Lee, "Youth of a Noble Birthright," in *Youth and the Church, No. 18* (Salt Lake City: Church of Jesus Christ of Latter-day Saints, 1945), Lee, *Youth and the Church* (Salt Lake City: Deseret News Press, 1945), 167–76.

28. Joseph Fielding Smith, *The Way to Perfection* (Salt Lake City: Deseret Book Co., 1931), in particular 97–111.

Church officials subsequently elevated the ban from practice/ policy to doctrine through an official First Presidency statement issued in August 1949 and signed by President George Albert Smith and his two counselors, J. Reuben Clark and David O. McKay. The statement proclaimed the ban as "a direct commandment from the Lord ... a doctrine ... to the effect that Negroes ... are not entitled to the priesthood at the present time."[29]

Throughout the 1950s and into the 1960s, church leaders continued to defend the ban, most notably, Joseph Fielding Smith.[30] Smith, moreover, expressed alarm over the emerging Civil Rights movement in the wake of the landmark 1954 Supreme Court decision *Brown v. Board of Education.* Smith lamented what he termed the "wave of 'non segregation' sweeping the country," expressing fear that "the doctrine of social equality" would result in racial intermarriage.[31]

Apostle Mark E. Petersen likewise lambasted the fledgling Civil Rights movement while affirming the legitimacy of the black priesthood denial. He presented his case in an address entitled "Race Problems—As they Affect the Church," delivered to LDS religious educators at a symposium at Brigham Young University in August 1954.[32] Apostle Ezra Taft Benson even more vigorously attacked the Civil Rights movement—asserting a direct link between the ongoing struggle for black equality and Communism.[33] "The Civil Rights movement," he declared, has been "fomented almost entirely by the communists,"[34] asserting that "Communists were using the

---

29. "LDS Church First Presidency Statement," Aug. 17, 1949, Church History Library, Church of Jesus Christ of Latter-day Saints, Salt Lake City. Published online, "Mormonism and the Negro," https://archive.org/details/mormonismandthenegro.

30. See Joseph Fielding Smith Jr., *Answers to Gospel Questions,* 5 vols. (Salt Lake City: Deseret Book Co., 1957–63); and Smith's *Doctrines of Salvation: Sermons and Writings of Joseph Fielding Smith,* 3 vols., comp. Bruce R. McConkie (Salt Lake City: Bookcraft, 1954–56).

31. Smith, as quoted in Wallace Turner, *The Mormon Establishment* (New York: Houghton Mifflin, 1966), 230–31.

32. Mark E. Petersen, "Race Problems—As They Affect the Church," address delivered to religious educators at Brigham Young University, Aug. 27, 1954, in Church History Library.

33. For a scholarly discussion of Benson as a foe of the Civil Rights movement, see Matthew L. Harris, "Martin Luther King, Civil Rights, and Perceptions of a 'Communist Conspiracy,'" in Matthew L. Harris, ed., *Thunder from the Right: Ezra Taft Benson in Mormonism and Politics* (Urbana: University of Illinois Press, 2019), 124–56.

34. *Deseret News,* Dec. 14, 1963.

Civil Rights movement to promote revolution and eventual take-over of this country."[35]

*

Lee likewise expressed skepticism concerning the ongoing Civil Rights movement, albeit less stridently. Lee warned about its potential adverse effects on the LDS Church. As a member of BYU's board of trustees, he favored completely barring blacks from attending the LDS institution. In 1960 he berated BYU president Ernest L. Wilkinson for allowing the admission of blacks, warning him of the negative consequences. "If a granddaughter of mine should ever go to the BYU and become engaged to a colored boy," Lee promised, "I would hold you responsible."[36]

In fact, Lee had reservations about allowing blacks into the church at all, which surfaced when some in the church wanted to send missionaries to Nigeria. Possible church activity in that nation was prompted by President McKay's dispatch of LaMar S. Williams, an employee of the Church Missionary Department, to Nigeria to determine the feasibility of proselytizing there. By this time, a grassroots LDS movement involving of some 5,000 black Nigerians was already under way. These self-styled black Latter-day Saints had organized, on their own, nearly 100 congregations. Their members, in turn, petitioned to be baptized as members of the church.[37] In response, McKay sent N. Eldon Tanner to Nigeria to dedicate "Nigeria for missionary work to be conducted as directed by the Lord through his Prophet."[38]

However, Lee opposed the Nigerian initiative, voicing his strongly held views in a November 1965 meeting of the First Presidency and Quorum of the Twelve. Lee took note of the obstacles encountered in this effort, specifically Williams's difficulty in securing a Nigerian visa. Lee suggested that the delay was "evidence

---

35. *Salt Lake Tribune*, Apr. 7, 1965.

36. Ernest L. Wilkinson, Diaries, Nov. 10, 1960, Ernest L. Wilkinson Papers, UA 1000, L. Tom Perry Special Collections, Harold B. Lee Library, Brigham Young University, Provo, Utah.

37. LaMar S. Williams to David O. McKay, undated letter cited in David Oman McKay, Diaries, David Oman McKay Papers, MS 668, Manuscripts Division, J. Willard Marriott Library, University of Utah, Salt Lake City.

38. N. Eldon Tanner, as quoted in McKay, Diaries, Jan. 10, 1963.

that the Lord is not ready to have this work done." Moreover, Lee questioned Williams's basic motives, disclosing that Williams on a previous occasion had advocated that "Negroes should receive at least the Aaronic Priesthood" to ensure missionary success in the country.[39] Lee feared that "a mission in Nigeria would open [the] door" to giving blacks the priesthood."[40]

Lee remained steadfast in his belief that the time was not right to lift the priesthood ban itself. This placed him at direct odds with Hugh B. Brown, who held the opposite view. As early as 1963, rumors circulated in the national press that the "top leadership" of the church was "seriously considering abandonment of its historic policy of discriminating against Negroes."[41] Specifically, Brown—a proponent of lifting the priesthood ban—announced that church leaders were "in the midst of a survey looking toward the possibility of admitting Negroes" in full fellowship. Brown publicly nudged McKay to lift the ban. Quoted in the pages of the *New York Times*, Brown proclaimed, "Believing as we do in divine revelation through the President of the church, we all await his decision."[42]

*

Although Brown's action failed to convince McKay to repeal the priesthood/temple ban, he succeeded in securing the approval of fellow general authorities to present a public statement affirming church support of civil rights.[43] The statement, read by Brown himself, was presented at the October 1963 general conference. "The

---

39. Minutes of First Presidency and Council of Twelve Meeting, Nov. 4, 1965, in McKay, Diaries, under date.

40. As suggested by Prince and Wright, *David O. McKay*, 92.

41. Wallace Turner, "Mormons Weigh Stand on Negroes," *New York Times,* June 7, 1963; *Newsweek,* June 17, 1963. According to the *New York Times,* December 28, 1965, the church as early as 1940 was contemplating a possible change in policy. A discussion of the origins is contained in Turner, *Mormon Establishment*, 218–45.

42. Turner, "Mormons Weigh Stand on Negroes."

43. Although the principal author of the statement, Brown secured the help of Sterling McMurrin, the outspoken advocate of equality for blacks both within and outside of the church who by this time had secured national stature as US Commissioner of Education in the John F. Kennedy administration. For a discussion of McMurrin's role in the crafting of the statement, see, Sterling McMurrin, "A Note on the 1963 Civil Rights Statement," *Dialogue: A Journal of Mormon Thought* 12, no. 2 (Summer 1979): 60–63, and McMurrin's interview with L. Jackson Newell, as cited in Sterling M. McMurrin and L. Jackson Newell, *Matters of Conscience: Conversations with Sterling McMurrin on Philosophy, Education, and Religion* (Salt Lake City: Signature Books, 1996), 200–201.

position of the Church ... on the matter of civil rights," the statement proclaimed, is "that there is in this Church no doctrine, belief, or practice that is intended to deny the employment of full civil rights by any person regardless of race, color, or creed," then adding, "it is a moral evil for any person or group of persons to deny any human being the right to gainful employment, to full educational opportunity, and to every privilege of citizenship." The statement concluded: "We call upon all men, everywhere, both within and outside of the Church, to commit themselves to the establishment of full civic equality for all of God's children."[44] The 1963 statement represented "the official Church position" on civil rights and was "personally approved by President McKay."

The civil rights statement notwithstanding, the church came under increasing attack for its perpetuation of the black priesthood ban from a spectrum of critics. Prominent church member Sterling McMurrin, a former US Commissioner of Education and longtime foe of the practice, repeatedly expressed his views to receptive audiences at yearly gatherings of the Salt Lake City chapter of the NAACP throughout the decade.[45] McMurrin was, in fact, a second cousin to Lee, whom he knew well and with whom he strongly disagreed with on this and other issues. A second prominent Latter-day Saint, Stewart Udall—US Secretary of Interior from 1961 to 1969—likewise publicly condemned the controversial church practice. Through the pages of the summer 1967 issue of *Dialogue: A Journal of Mormon Thought*, Udall dismissed the ban as "a social and institutional practice having no real sanction in Mormon thought."[46]

From outside the Mormon community, protests condemning the church's policy were directed against BYU and often staged by black athletes from colleges and universities with which the LDS-owned school had athletic relations. Such protests commenced in the spring

---

44. As quoted in Hugh B. Brown, *One Hundred Thirty-third Semi-annual Conference Report of the Church of Jesus Christ of Latter-day Saints* (Salt Lake City: Church of Jesus Christ of Latter-day Saints, 1963), 91.

45. *Chicago Sun-Times*, Apr. 5, 1965. Sterling M. McMurrin, "The Negros Among the Mormons," a speech given June 21, 1968, reprinted by the Salt Lake Chapter of the NAACP, 1968.

46. Stewart Udall, "Letter to the Editor," *Dialogue: A Journal of Mormon Thought* 2, no. 2 (Summer 1967): 5–7.

of 1968 and continued throughout the remainder of the decade. The schools involved included the University of Texas at El Paso, San Jose State University, Stanford University, and the University of Washington.[47] Such unrest prompted *Sports Illustrated* to characterize BYU as a school under siege, "As much as the [BYU] Cougars would like to ignore [the protests] they have grown in intensity to the point where they have almost transcended all else."[48]

Such activity notwithstanding, Lee held fast in affirming the church's ban. He remained convinced that "the ban was doctrinally fixed."[49] In an address delivered to seminary and institute faculty at BYU, he dismissed as "utterly silly" the question: "How long is it going to be before the Church changes its policy with respect to the Negro?" Instead, he deflected, asking, "How long is it going to be before the Lord (not the Church) changes His (not its) policy?", and responded, "When there is anything different from that which the Lord has told us already, He will reveal it to his prophet and no one else."[50]

*

Lee's commitment to the ban brought him once more into direct conflict with First Presidency counselor Brown. In late 1969, Brown renewed his decade-long crusade to rid the church of the ban. The ban "had no justification as far as the scriptures are concerned," Brown asserted.[51]

Accordingly, in November 1969, Brown lobbied for approval from the Twelve to abolish the ban—ultimately gaining support from a majority of that body. Absent from the deliberations were Lee and First Presidency counselor Alvin R. Dyer—who, like Lee,

---

47. *New York Times*, Apr. 13, 1968; *Fort Myers (Florida) New Press*, Apr. 14, 1968; *Arizona Daily Star*, Apr. 14, 1968. Gary James Bergera, "'This Time of Crisis': The Race-Based Protests Anti-BYU Athletic Protests of 1958–1971," *Utah Historical Quarterly* 81 no. 3 (Summer 2013): 204–29, provides a thorough analysis of the protests.

48. William F. Reed, "The Other Side of the 'Y,'" *Sports Illustrated*, Jan. 26, 1970.

49. These are the words of Edward L. Kimball in *Lengthen Your Stride: The Presidency of Spencer W. Kimball* (Salt Lake City: Deseret Book Co., 2003), 294.

50. Harold B. Lee, "The Place of the Living Prophet, Seer, and Revelator," an address to seminary and institute faculty, Brigham Young University, July 8, 1964, reprinted in *Stand Ye in Holy Places: Selected Sermons and Writings of President Harold B. Lee* (Salt Lake City: Deseret Book Co., 1974), 159.

51. As quoted in D. Michael Quinn, *The Mormon Hierarchy: Extensions of Power* (Salt Lake City: Signature Books, 1997), 13.

was an ardent supporter of the ban.[52] Both men were away from Utah on church assignment. Also missing were President McKay—who was ill—and Joseph Fielding Smith.

Upon returning to Salt Lake City a few days later, Lee moved quickly to nullify Brown's initiative, persuading a majority of the Twelve along with First Presidency counselor N. Eldon Tanner to withdraw their support for lifting the ban. Lee, realizing that a policy statement would be necessary to clear up the confusion caused by Brown, "spent several days documenting his own thinking on this weighty subject."[53] Following that, "[Lee] then asked G. Homer Durham and Neal A. Maxwell, prominent educators, to do likewise. Placing their texts with his own, [Lee] delivered the three approaches to Apostle Gordon B. Hinckley and asked him to formulate out of their combined thinking a clarifying statement that could be read by critics as wells as members of the Church."[54]

The official 1969 church statement reaffirmed the ban as doctrine. Dated December 15, 1969, the document was signed by just two members of the First Presidency—Brown and Tanner. Failing to sign it was the ailing McKay, who died a month later on January 18, 1970. Two other members of the First Presidency also did not sign the document: Joseph Fielding Smith and Alvin R. Dyer.

Brown signed the document only under strong pressure from Lee, who, by this time, had emerged as the dominant figure within the church hierarchy. Brown reportedly wept when he affixed his signature, and later lamented that "he was forced to do so in order to maintain the appearance of unanimity in the Church." Before signing, and as a compromise, Brown insisted that the document reaffirm the church's support for civil rights.[55]

The official statement reaffirmed the legitimacy of the ban: "From the beginning of this dispensation, Joseph Smith and all succeeding president of the Church have taught that Negroes ... were not yet to receive the priesthood for reasons which we believe are

---

52. Reflective of Dyer's views was the address he delivered in 1959 as European Mission president entitled "For What Purpose?," March 18, 1961.

53. Goates, 379.

54. As recalled by Goates, 380.

55. As noted by Brown's grandson Edwin B. Firmage in *An Abundant Life: The Memoirs of Hugh B. Brown* (Salt Lake City: Signature Books, 1988), 142–43.

known to God, but which He has not made fully known to man." Then, quoting McKay, the statement continued that this "seeming discrimination by the Church toward the Negro is not something which originated with man; but goes back into the beginning with God," adding that "this plan antedates man's mortal existence extending back to man's pre-existent state." It concluded with McKay's promise: "Sometime in God's eternal plan, the Negro will be given the right to hold the priesthood."[56]

Brown had the final word, stating in a December 25 *Salt Lake Tribune* article that the priesthood ban "will change in the not too distant future."[57] This statement angered Lee, who, in private, berated Brown for "talking too much."[58]

Given Lee's action, the LDS Church's ban on black priesthood ordination and temple ordinances continued as fixed doctrine. His commitment to the ban was manifested in a vow, made to oldest daughter, Maurine: "My daddy said that as long as he's alive, [blacks] will never hold the priesthood."[59]

*

Outside of his church responsibilities, Lee endured the tragic loss of two immediate family members: his wife, Fern, and oldest daughter, Maurine. Their deaths occurred within a three-year period.

Fern Tanner Lee, always in frail health, had endured a rigorous schedule of travel over the years accompanying her husband to numerous destinations in the United States and abroad. Their most recent trip was to the South Pacific from May to June 1961. Fern's decline commenced in early January 1962 with recurring fainting spells and continued over the following months. In April she was briefly hospitalized after becoming unconscious and suffering a slight concussion.[60]

---

56. "Statement of the First Presidency," Dec. 15, 1969, in Church News section, *Deseret News,* Jan. 10, 1970.

57. "LDS Leader Says Curb on Priesthood to Ease," *Salt Lake Tribune,* Dec. 25, 1969.

58. As reported in Ernest L. Wilkinson, Memorandum, Dec. 27, 1969, in Wilkinson, Diaries, under date.

59. Maurine Lee Wilkins, as quoted in Ramona Bernhard, Interview, Dec. 5, 1998. Original interview in possession of Gregory A. Prince, who interviewed Bernhard, a close friend of Wilkins.

60. Goates, 343–44; Gibbons, 393–95.

A second, lengthier hospitalization in early September 1962 led to the more precise diagnosis that, beyond serious hypertension, she was suffering from periodic brain clots. These, in turn, caused "pain, nausea, and feelings of despondency." Medication and injections provided little relief. Shortly thereafter she appeared to recover; release from the hospital appeared imminent. But then she suffered a massive cerebral hemorrhage. Her condition worsened, and she died on September 24, 1962.[61] Fern Tanner Lee was sixty-five years old.

The next few months proved particularly difficult for the grieving widower, living alone in what had been Fern's dream home on Penrose Drive. Harold's sister Verda, sensitive to her brother's situation, moved into the his home along with her husband, Charles, to provide companionship and a semblance of family life. Harold, however, suffered "spells of nervous tension and depression, sometimes accompanied by tears." His despondency became worse on November 14, Fern's birthday and their wedding anniversary, which he recalled as "a most difficult day of memories."[62]

Lee resumed his apostolic duties, hoping that being anxiously engaged would revive his spirits. President McKay dispatched Lee to Germany accompanied by Walter Stover, who noted that "at the time [Lee] was in deep sorrow for the loss of his beloved eternal companion." Stover further recalled seeing him "weep on many occasions ... it was very difficult for me to cheer him up."[63] Lee continued to struggle with depression that dominated his "waking hours and troubled his dreams" throughout the rest of 1962.[64]

*

Finally, in January 1963, Lee's despondency began to dissipate, the result of two developments. The first involved advice from John A. Sibley, a non-Mormon friend on the board of Equitable Life Assurance Society. Sibley, who had recently lost his own wife, shared his own experience: "This is the most severe test you will ever be confronted with in your life. If you can meet and surmount its test, there is nothing else in life you cannot meet and

61. Gibbons, 395–96; Goates, 343–46.
62. As recalled by Lee, in Gibbons, 396–97.
63. As recalled by Walter Stover, in Goates, 549.
64. As noted by Gibbons, 397.

surmount." As Lee recalled, "Strangely, this bit of wisdom from this fine man gave me comfort."[65]

The second development involved Lee's decision to remarry. In coming to this seemingly quick decision, a mere three months following Fern's death, he took to heart the admonition of his late wife. Aware of her own frail heath, Fern had told her husband that if she preceded him in death, he should remarry as soon as possible.[66]

Lee formulated a list of the qualities he desired in a new companion. Preferably, she should be near his own age, someone whom Fern had known, and someone who had not been previously married. A woman possessing these qualities was Freda Joan Jensen, a well-known local educator who served as the supervisor of primary education for the Jordan School District. Lee was well acquainted with Joan (as she preferred to be called) given her church service on the general boards of both the Primary and Young Women's Mutual Improvement Association. At sixty-five, she had never married. She had been engaged to Ray Beck, a young widower with three children, but Beck had died suddenly just two weeks before their scheduled wedding. She never again considered marriage until Lee approached her. The two married in the Salt Lake Temple on June 17, 1963, the ceremony performed by President McKay, with Marion G. Romney and Henry D. Moyle as witnesses.[67]

Two years later, Lee was confronted with the sudden death of his oldest daughter, Maureen, in August 1965. She died of a lung embolism while pregnant with her fifth child, making it a double tragedy. Maureen, just forty years old, left behind her husband, Ernest Wilkins, and four children. Lee vented in his journal: "My heart is broken as I contemplate the passing of my darling 'Sunshine' and the great need that Ernie and her family of four little ones have for her." Lee added, "I was so completely overwhelmed and could hardly control myself physically, or emotionally when I saw the little motherless family."[68] "Somehow," he confided, "I am unable to shake off this the latest, shattering blow. Only God can help me."[69] Lee

---

65. As recalled by Lee, in Goates, 350–51.
66. Gibbons, 398.
67. Goates, 357–62.
68. Lee, as quoted from his diary, Goates, 352–53.
69. Lee, as quoted from his diary, Gibbons, 404.

confessed to suffering from "the shock and the strain of my darling Maurine's passing," adding that it compounds "my sorrow in losing Fern three years ago."[70]

*

Meanwhile, Lee confronted a series of health problems of his own—the result of aging combined with the pressures of his apostolic responsibilities.

In March 1963, Lee underwent minor surgery for a hernia repair. The following year he contracted a viral infection while on a trip in the eastern United States. This condition left him so weak that he was unable to discharge his duties. A complete physical examination following his return determined that he was suffering from a bleeding ulcer.[71] In January 1966 he was hospitalized for two ailments: feelings of inertia (the result of unusually low blood levels) and persistent headaches. For the first condition, he was given a series of blood transfusions. For the headaches, however, no cure could be found. The following year, in March 1967, Lee was hospitalized again with low blood levels and again given a blood transfusion along with iron shots. Lee's doctor admonished him to slow down—advice Lee ignored.[72]

Lee resumed his whirlwind schedule of travel on behalf the church, traveling in late March 1967 to New York City. There he experienced faintness and extreme pain. He returned to Utah and was rushed to a local hospital where he went through a series of tests that indicated major surgery was required. One-half of his stomach was removed in a thirteen-hour operation upon discovering "a large ulcer in [his] duodenal bulb." Fortunately, no malignancy was found, although he lost fifteen pounds during his hospital stay. By April 27, Lee felt sufficiently recovered to resume his schedule. As he remarked, "I am amazed at no pain in my digestive system, and my headaches [have been] reduced to a minimum. The Lord, indeed, has been good to me."[73] Lee's doctor advised him to reduce his

---

70. Lee, as quoted in Goates, 352.
71. Goates, 385.
72. Gibbons, 406–407.
73. Lee, as quoted in Gibbons, 498.

workload, specifically to "do only half a man's work rather than the work of ten men as in the past."[74]

A year later, in April 1968, Lee was yet again compelled to scale back his church duties due to a severe lung infection. Over the course of the following year, he continued to suffer from "unexplained exhaustion." And in September 1969 he was hospitalized once more. Tests revealed that his left kidney was not functioning properly because of a large kidney stone blockage, which was ultimately removed. Lee "struggled to rise above the pain and discomfort and worrisome anxieties" as he convalesced in the hospital over the following three weeks.[75] By early November 1969, he regained sufficient strength to "take my first steps into full-scale activity."[76]

*

The 1960s proved a significant period of transition for Lee and the LDS Church at large. The church experienced unprecedented growth in its total membership, from 1,690,000 in 1960 to 2,931,000 by 1970, an increase of over 1.2 million—an annual growth rate of 5–6 percent per year. Internationally, the church's growth occurred in accordance with McKay's vow to keep members in their own countries, thus abandoning the church's historic policy of "Gathering to Zion."

Lee played a central role in the church's response to growth through the implementation of correlation, which allowed for a more efficient, streamlined church under priesthood authority. Correlation eliminated what one scholar has characterized as "fragmentation, overlap, and dysfunction [that] had grown almost unmanageable."[77] It also allowed for the preservation of "doctrinal integrity, the authority of the priesthood hierarchy, and the emphasis on right behavior that had become so important to Mormonism."[78] Yet another important aspect of correlation was its "theological emphasis on strict moral behavior and adherence to authority and not theological innovation."[79] Thus it "downplayed theology in favor of a

---

74. James F. Orme, as quoted in Goates, 388.

75. Gibbons, 408–10; Goates, 388–90.

76. Lee, as quoted in Gibbons, 410.

77. The words of Matthew Bowman in *The Mormon People: The Making of an American Faith* (New York: Random House, 2012), 194.

78. Again, quoting Bowman, *Mormon People*, 193.

79. As further stated by Bowman, *Mormon People*, 197.

strict moral code and conservative doctrinal beliefs"—all very much in line with Lee's own thinking.[80]

Correlation conformed with Lee's other major action during the 1960s: his success in preserving the church's priesthood and temple ban. In reaffirming the ban's status as doctrine, Lee prevailed over those in the hierarchy who lobbied to lift the ban as well as critics both within and outside the LDS community.

Lee's success in perpetuating the ban, however, did not end debate concerning its legitimacy, as he would discover as he moved up in the hierarchy as a member of the First Presidency and ultimately as church president. He would face other major challenges and controversies as well over the next four years as he took charge of church affairs.

80. Bowman, *Mormon People*, 191.

CHAPTER EIGHT

TAKING CHARGE
1970-72

Throughout the two and a half years from January 1970 to July 1972, Lee found himself busier than ever as he took charge of the day-to-day running of the Church of Jesus Christ of Latter-day Saints. He assumed a myriad of new duties and responsibilities resulting from his elevation to the First Presidency in January 1970. In fact, the newly installed first counselor took on the majority of duties traditionally given to the church president due to Joseph Fielding Smith's frail heath and advanced age. Lee became the de facto church president.

Thus, Lee filled an ambitious schedule of travel both within the United States and abroad in response to the church's continued growth and evolution as an international movement. Through his sermons, he continued to stress doctrinal orthodoxy combined with strict obedience as essential safeguards against the corrupting influence of secularism. Lee led the church with both vigor and energy, appearing much younger than a man in his early seventies. However, his robust demeanor masked a host of chronic health problems, which worsened over time.

*

The death of ninety-six-year-old David O. McKay on January 18, 1970, marked the end of an epic twenty-year tenure during which he presided over a church experiencing an unprecedented increase in membership and geographic expansion.

McKay's death was not unexpected; he had suffered from declining health over much of the previous decade, including diminishing mental capacity. As early as 1965, McKay's longtime personal secretary,

Clare Middlemiss, lamented that the LDS leader was "slowly deteriorating," while "several general authorities" opined that McKay was "senile." Others close to him observed that he appeared "somewhat confused" in meetings and thus "had to be guided by his counselors."[1]

All of this created a "leadership vacuum" into which several "strong willed" general authorities stepped in to promote an array of "pet agendas."[2] For Lee, the time proved ideal for pushing ahead with churchwide correlation. Likewise, other church leaders championed their own sometimes controversial agendas. First Presidency counselor Henry Moyle, through his ambitious building program, placed the church in temporary economic straits. Moyle also aggressively advocated an innovative proselytizing program known as "baseball baptisms," which produced an avalanche of new converts. Moyle's initiative was ultimately abandoned when it was discovered that many of the young converts "had no idea they were considered Mormons or were unhappy with the fact."[3] Even more controversial were Apostle Ezra Taft Benson's political actions, which involved vigorously promoting the conspiracy theories of the ultra-right-wing John Birch Society while simultaneously seeking reentry into the political arena as George C. Wallace's vice-presidential running mate on his segregationist American Independent Party ticket in 1968.[4] On the opposite end of the ideological spectrum, Hugh B. Brown lobbied for the lifting of the black priesthood/temple ban, a failed effort that produced the opposite result—a reaffirmation of the ban through the 1969 official First Presidency statement, which Lee himself had helped to craft.[5]

Such disorder underscored the need to restore strong, stable leadership to the First Presidency. This, in turn, generated questions as

---

1. All three of the above assessments of McKay are quoted in D. Michael Quinn, *The Mormon Hierarchy: Extensions of Power* (Salt Lake City: Signature Books, 1997), 54.

2. As noted by Quinn, *Mormon Hierarchy: Extensions of Power,* 55.

3. As noted in Matthew Bowman, *The Mormon People: The Making of an American Faith* (New York: Random House, 2012), 198–200.

4. For two extensive discussions of Benson's political activities, see Matthew L. Harris, ed., *Thunder from the Right: Ezra Taft Benson in Mormonism and Politics* (Urbana: University of Illinois Press, 2019), and Harris, *Watchman on the Tower: Ezra Taft Benson and the Making of the Mormon Right* (Salt Lake City: University of Utah Press, 2020).

5. For a personal perspective on this effort, see Edwin B. Firmage, ed., *An Abundant Life: The Memoirs of Hugh B. Brown* (Salt Lake City: Signature Books, 1999).

to the suitability of Joseph Fielding Smith as McKay's successor. At ninety-three, the aging, frail Smith was in declining health and diminishing mental capacity. Smith's health sparked rumors that church leaders were giving serious consideration to bypassing Smith in favor of the younger, more vigorous Lee.

Smith was alarmed by this breach of protocol and made his case directly to Lee in a face-to-face meeting, accompanied by his sixty-seven-year-old wife, Jessie Evans Smith.

A force in her own right, Jessie Evans Smith strongly argued on behalf of her husband. A dynamic, charismatic personality, Jessie, prior to her marriage, had gained local fame as a vocalist performing with the American Light Opera Company. She preferred a career in business and politics, but in 1938, at age thirty-seven, married the recently widowed Smith. (Smith had fathered eleven children with two wives, both of whom had died before turning fifty.) Jessie Evans embraced her new status as the wife of a ranking general authority while also serving as a prominent member of the Mormon Tabernacle Choir.

Jessie Evans Smith took the lead in affirming her husband's right to be church president, revealing to Lee an 1887 letter written by Wilford Woodruff to then-apostle Heber J. Grant following the death of church president John Taylor. Woodruff had affirmed his legitimate right as president of the Twelve to assume the office of church president, which was in question at the time. In response to the question *Who becomes president of the church when the sitting president dies?* Woodruff asserted, "It is the President of the Twelve Apostles. And he is virtually as much the President of the Church while presiding over twelve men as he is when organized as the Presidency of the Church while presiding over two men."[6]

Jessie Evans Smith told Lee that "if Joseph Fielding Smith were sustained as President, he wanted Elder Lee to be 'by his side' which Elder Lee interpreted to mean Smith wanted him to serve as a counselor in the First Presidency."[7]

Lee affirmed his support for Joseph Fielding Smith as church president, stating, "It would require a revelation from ... God ... before I would give my vote or influence to depart from the paths

---

6. As quoted in Goates, 403–404.
7. As quoted in Goates, 403.

followed by the Apostles since the organization of the Church and followed by the inspiration of Almighty God."[8]

*

Joseph Fielding Smith was subsequently sustained as the tenth president of the LDS Church despite "his age and poor health."[9] Lee was appointed as first counselor and N. Eldon Tanner remained second counselor. Released from the First Presidency were Hugh B. Brown, Alvin R. Dyer, and Thorpe B. Isaacson. Brown returned to the Quorum of the Twelve; Dyer and Isaacson reverted to their prior status as assistants to the Twelve. Appointed to fill the vacancy in the Twelve created by Lee's elevation was Boyd K. Packer, currently an assistant to the Twelve and longtime Lee protégé.

As church president, the aging Smith was given one major duty, overseeing the temples and related matters. Even in this limited task, Smith was assisted by Lee.[10]

On the other hand, Lee assumed a myriad of major responsibilities. Among these was overseeing church education, budgeting, finance, management systems (computer technology), and communications—specifically, all church-owned media including KSL radio and television, Bonneville International Corporation, and the *Deseret News*. Lee also assumed executive responsibilities over certain church-owned or controlled corporations: Zion's Securities Corporation, ZCMI Department Store, Utah–Idaho Sugar Company, Hotel Utah, Beneficial Life Insurance, Deseret Book Company, and Deseret Management Corporation—the latter a holding company. Finally, Lee assumed oversight of the Relief Society and Primary auxiliaries, as well as church personnel.[11]

Such responsibilities notwithstanding, Lee continued to push ahead with correlation. He assigned Apostle Thomas S. Monson a major role in maintaining "constant surveillance" over correlation's "many details."[12]

Lee retained his position as president of the Twelve although Spencer W. Kimball, as acting president of the Twelve, assumed a

---

8. As quoted in Goates, 404.
9. Smith, as described by Goates, 404.
10. Gibbons, 422.
11. Gibbons, 422.
12. Gibbons, 422.

number of the duties normally assigned to the president, somewhat easing Lee's burden.

Thus, Lee served as de facto leader of the LDS Church over the following two and a half years. Indeed, Smith acknowledged this fact when he stated, "I don't know how I could get along without Brother Lee, my strong right arm, who supports and defends me." Smith further explained that Lee's "knowledge and understanding of the church and its needs is not surpassed by any man."[13]

*

Among Lee's most immediate concerns was beefing up church security, given continuing outside threats directed at the church in the wake of its reaffirmation of the priesthood/temple denial as doctrine.

To protest the church's anti-black doctrine, Stanford University terminated all future athletic competitions with BYU in November 1969.[14] Worse was a near riot in Fort Collins during a February 1970 basketball game between BYU and Colorado State. The melee commenced with a group of black CSU students shouting at BYU basketball players. The situation escalated when eggs, an iron projectile, and ultimately a lighted torch were hurled onto the playing floor. Fights broke out in the stands between students from the rival schools. The riot ended when local police were summoned.[15]

Threatening the LDS Church itself was Jerry Rubin, an anti-establishment radical who had gained fame as one of the 1968 Chicago Seven. During the course of a fiery February 1970 speech delivered to a University of Utah audience, Rubin declared, "We will either integrate the Mormon Church or we will destroy it."[16]

More disconcerting was a series of three bomb threats made during the April 1970 LDS general conference. Two of these were called in to church officials prior to the opening of the conference's general session. A third telephone threat came during the Sunday afternoon session on April 5 when Lee was presiding. Lee was delivered a note indicating that an anonymous call had been received "stating that a bomb would go off during that session." In response,

---

13. As quoted by Joseph Fielding Smith, in Goates, 409 and 411.
14. Gibbons, 423.
15. Gibbons, 423.
16. Gibbons, 423.

Lee calmly said to the audience: "There is no bomb in here, relax." The session continued without incident.[17]

Such threats prompted officials to increase security on church property, taking to heart Lee's oft-quoted scriptural admonition, "If ye are prepared, ye shall not fear."[18] Up to that time, church security consisted of "a few men … practically all of whom lacked professional security training" and were "little more than night watchmen." The Church Administration Building itself lacked even a receptionist, and thus was open to anyone who entered, regardless of their intentions. Even more alarming was the lack of protection for the general authorities.[19]

Measures were taken to remedy such deficiencies. The size of the security force was increased, augmented with men who had professional training in law enforcement. Video cameras were placed in strategic places throughout church headquarters buildings, and security personnel were equipped with walkie-talkies. To control entry into church headquarters, a male receptionist, trained in law enforcement, screened out any who did not have a legitimate reason to be in the building. As a further safety measure, bullet-proof glass was installed in the windows on the main floor of the administration building.[20]

*

Seeking "to put the Church on the offensive in the arena of public opinion," Lee quickly moved forward with a number of organizational changes. He was acutely aware that the church's image was at "such low ebb" because of "the negro priesthood issue," as he termed it. He hoped to counter the "emerging groundswells of anti-Mormon sentiment."[21]

Acting on Lee's instructions, church officials established the Department of Public Communications, ultimately named the Department of Public Affairs. Lee chose Wendell J. Ashton, an executive in a Salt Lake City-based advertising and public relations firm as director of the department. Lee saw Ashton as possessing

---

17. Lee, as quoted in Goates, 413–14.
18. Lee, as quoted in Gibbons, 424.
19. Gibbons, 424.
20. Gibbons, 425.
21. Lee, as quoted in Gibbons, 426.

"the natural ability to greatly improve public relations and to communicate appropriately whenever the occasion requires."[22]

Seeking to counter the public image of the church as racist, Lee authorized creation of the Genesis Group in June 1971, offering to the church's black members a limited ecclesiastical independence. Lee stated that he had "spent considerable time in [a] temple meeting of the First Presidency and the Quorum of the Twelve considering what could be done with our black members locally who want to be more fully worshipped."[23]

Actually, the major impetus for Genesis came not from Lee, but from three African American Latter-day Saint men: Ruffin Bridgeforth, Darius Gray, and Eugene Orr, who together petitioned church headquarters to form a special organization for Black Latter-day Saints in the Salt Lake City area. In its organization, the Genesis Group served as an auxiliary unit of the Liberty Stake in Salt Lake City and met monthly to share testimony and to provide outreach to the Black LDS community. Apostles Gordon B. Hinckley, Thomas S. Monson, and Boyd K. Packer oversaw the group's activities and provided edification and instruction.[24]

Lee made clear what he perceived as the group's proper, limited role, stating, "My feelings are that ... we should extend to our black brethren every blessing up to the holding of the priesthood," carefully and ambiguously adding, "and then the Lord will show us the next step."[25] By contrast, Genesis made clear that its "main objective was to get the priesthood." In an early meeting of Genesis, the three apostles overseeing the group were reportedly told that blacks wanted the priesthood. When pressed, the apostles claimed that "the First Presidency and the Twelve [had] prayed about whether Black members ... should hold the Priesthood" but that the "First Presidency and the Twelve were not in agreement

22. Lee, as quoted in Gibbons, 431.

23. As stated by Lee, in Goates, 380.

24. Jesse L. Embry, *Black Saints in a White Church* (Salt Lake City: Signature Books, 1994), 182–91; and Armand L. Mauss, *All Abraham's Children: Changing Mormon Conceptions of Race and Lineage* (Urbana: University of Illinois Press, 2003), 235–36, provide an overview of the formation of the Genesis Group.

25. As stated by Lee, in Goates, 380.

on the question."[26] Thus black priesthood ordination and temple participation remained unresolved.

Another organizational change pushed forward by Lee involved restructuring the duties of the members of the Quorum of the Twelve. The process commenced in the spring of 1971 in response to an in-depth study of church operations ordered by Lee. The report questioned the efficiency of having members of the Twelve do staff work at the expense of broader policymaking functions—the latter increasingly important as the church continued to expand. Implementing the report's recommendations, the Quorum was relived of daily supervision of various church departments and other managerial tasks. The assistants to the Twelve and the First Council of Seventy assumed day-to-day oversight of the various church departments. The Twelve's primary responsibilities included planning, policy making, and exercising control over the funds being budgeted. Members of the Twelve served as advisors rather than as managers.[27]

Further improving operational efficiency, Lee authorized the establishment of the Department of Internal Communications in 1972, under the supervision of J. Thomas Fyans, an assistant to the Twelve. This department took over the functions of the Correlation Committee and assumed responsibility for planning, preparing, translating, printing, and distributing all communications, instructional materials, and periodicals for church members worldwide. The department brought together translation and distribution services, all church publications, editorial services, and curriculum planning. To facilitate this process, an elaborate instructional development program was established to create teaching materials for all the church's auxiliaries and other organizations.[28]

The Church Historical Department was also established in 1972, superseding what had been called the Church Historian's Office. Creation of the new department came in response to two developments: (1) the church's vast and growing archival holdings, and

---

26. This according to H. Michael Marquardt's interview with Eugene Orr, Nov. 7, 14, 1971, box 6, fd. 3, H. Michael Marquardt Papers, Manuscripts Division, J. Willard Marriott Library, University of Utah, Salt Lake City.

27. Goates, 436–38.

28. James B. Allen and Glen M. Leonard, *The Story of the Latter-day Saints*, 2nd ed. (Salt Lake City: Deseret Book Co., 1992), 607.

(2) the need for the church itself to engage in more research and writing. Under managing director Howard W. Hunter (an apostle) and his successor, Alvin R. Dyer, the department was divided into three major divisions, and the staff was enlarged with the hiring of a corps of professionally trained historians. Church Archives, under the direction of Earl E. Olson, was responsible for acquiring, storing, and managing historical documents and records. The Church Library, under Donald T. Schmidt, took charge of acquiring and making available to church authorities and the general public printed church materials. The History Division under Leonard J. Arrington, as Church Historian, oversaw the writing and publishing of church history. Arrington was the only non-general-authority ever sustained and set apart as official Church Historian.[29]

*

Meanwhile, Lee was compelled to travel abroad in response to the church's increasing growth outside the United States and continuing evolution into an international organization.

Lee's April 1971 journey took him, along with wife, Joan, to Asia—his second trip to the region, the first having taken place some seventeen years earlier in 1954. The number of Asian Latter-day Saints had increased substantially since that time. In Korea, the church consisted of some five thousand members, considerably more than the few dozen in 1954. Such growth caused Lee to boast, "Bringing the gospel to the Korean people is like sowing good seed on fertile ground."[30] In Taiwan, Lee encountered a total membership of 5,100; he reported the island nation to be "surprisingly clean and colorful and measurably prosperous."[31] In Hong Kong, he found that the church had grown from just ten members in 1954 to over five thousand. In Japan, he saw that membership had grown even more dramatically, from eight hundred in 1953 to twenty thousand. Underscoring such growth was the formation of the Tokyo Stake a year earlier—the first LDS stake in Asia.

---

29. For two accounts describing the establishment and evolving role of the Church Historical Department, see Leonard J. Arrington, *Adventures of a Church Historian* (Urbana: University of Illinois Press, 1998); and Gregory A. Prince, *Leonard Arrington and the Writing of Mormon History* (Salt Lake City: University of Utah Press, 2016).

30. Lee, as quoted in Goates, 425.

31. Lee, as quoted in Goates, 424–25.

Traveling back to Salt Lake City, Lee stopped briefly in Hawaii where he addressed students at the Church College of Hawaii (later BYU-Hawaii). There he delivered a sermon counseling "students against interracial marriages." Such advice reflected Lee's aversion to all such "mixed" marriages. At the same time, he urged LDS students from various Pacific Rim nations "to return to their home lands, rather than remaining in Hawaii."[32]

In general, Lee summed up Mormonism's presence in Asia as follows: "The growth of the Church in the Orient is most exciting, not only in numbers but also in strength of organization and leadership." He characterized Asia as "a sleeping giant, just awakening to the immense possibilities available through ... the Gospel."[33]

Lee's next journey abroad in August 1971 took him to Manchester, England, again accompanied by Joan. Joining the Lees was an increasingly frail Joseph Fielding Smith, who presided over the church's first area conference. A primary purpose of the conference was to stress the church's international focus, assuring members abroad that the leaders in Utah were anxious to address their particular needs and concerns.[34] Underscoring this purpose, seven members of the Quorum of the Twelve joined Presidents Smith and Lee at the conference. Another noteworthy attendee was Russell M. Nelson, general superintendent of the Sunday School and a future church president. The general sessions of the conference attracted approximately ten thousand Latter-day Saint faithful, who traveled from throughout England.[35]

In his keynote sermon, Lee affirmed that "the answers to life's complex problems could be found through adherence to the gospel," and further admonished his audience "to guard against the intrusion of Satanic influences in their lives."[36] The conference generated favorable coverage in the British media, specifically the *Manchester Guardian* and the *London Times*. The BBC aired a fifty-minute documentary on the church. Lee was pleased with the "quite fair

---

32. Lee, as quoted in Goates, 427.
33. As quoted in Goates, 426–27.
34. As stated by Gibbons, 442.
35. Goates, 422–23.
36. Lee, as quoted in Gibbons, 448.

and positive" coverage.[37] Thus ran the church's first area conference, followed in subsequent years by area conferences throughout Asia, South America, and Europe.

*

Lee witnessed and/or was a party to a number of less positive events during this period as well.

The unexpected death of sixty-five-year-old apostle Richard L. Evans in October 1971 was tragic. Evans was well-known to church members as the beloved longtime host of the church's weekly radio and television program *Music and the Spoken Word*. Evans's sudden death was caused by an attack of encephalitis—a fatal disease affecting the brain.[38] Replacing Evans in the Twelve was Marvin J. Ashton, an assistant to the Twelve and director of Church Social Services. The fifty-six-year-old Ashton was a native of Salt Lake City and the son of Marvin O. Ashton, himself a one-time general authority. Marvin J. had been a businessman prior to his church service.

Equally shocking was the death of sixty-six-year-old Jessie Evans Smith in August 1971. The beloved, strong-willed, robust wife of Joseph Fielding Smith died of heart failure. Her death left Smith, ninety-three years old, in a state of shock and depression. While Smith attended the Manchester area conference, members of his family moved his belongings to the home of his son-in-law, Bruce R. McConkie.[39]

Smith further scaled back his activities as president, leaving counselors Lee and Tanner to jointly conduct the October 1971 general conference. Smith did manage to deliver a brief keynote address in which he acknowledged their help: "May I express before you the profound appreciation of the two great men who stand beside me." He characterized Lee as "a spiritual giant with faith like that of Enoch. He has the spirit of revelation and magnifies his calling as a prophet, seer, and revelator."[40]

Creating further uncertainty were life-threatening health problems suffered by Spencer W. Kimball. Having been treated for cancer

---

37. Lee, as quoted in Goates, 423.
38. Goates, 430–32.
39. Goates, 412.
40. Joseph Fielding Smith, as quoted in Gibbons, 451.

some fourteen years earlier, Kimball experienced a relapse. Worse, Kimball was found to be afflicted with serious heart problems resulting from a blocked coronary artery. Kimball's heart specialist, Russell M. Nelson, recommended open-heart surgery. However, before such surgery could be performed, six weeks of cobalt treatment were required to arrest the growth of the cancer in his throat.[41]

Kimball expressed strong reluctance about going through the high-risk surgery, confiding his concerns to Lee. In response, Lee reportedly rose to his feet, pounded his fist on his desk, and exclaimed, "Spencer, you have been called! You are not going to die! You are to do everything you need to do in order to care for yourself and continue to live."[42] Kimball took Lee's advice to heart. Finally, on April 12, 1972, Nelson successfully performed open-heart surgery on Kimball, a four-and-a-half-hour procedure. Nelson remarked that he "felt like a baseball pitcher who had just thrown a perfect game."[43] Such success ensured the survival of Kimball, who went on to become church president. Indeed, Nelson himself became president in 2018.

Meanwhile, Lee continued to shoulder the burdens of overall leadership. At the end of his first year as Smith's counselor, Lee mused: "This past year has been … the most demanding year of my life because of my call … bringing never-ending responsibilities and problems." But then he carefully added, "Through it all there has been a continuing awareness of the influence of spiritual guidance and heavenly direction."[44] One year later, he further commented: "The continual round of meetings and interviews left me no time to tend to my personal affairs, much less give some thought to my preparation for the forthcoming conference sessions."[45]

Through all this, Lee had to deal with his own health problems, the most persistent being migraine headaches exacerbated by heavy administrative duties. As he wrote on January 13, 1972, "Following the temple meeting today I became ill with an intensely severe

41. For a discussion of Kimball's ordeal, see Edward L. Kimball and Andrew W. Kimball, *Spencer W. Kimball* (Salt Lake City: Bookcraft, 1977), 394–99.

42. Lee, as quoted in Goates, 418.

43. Russell M. Nelson, as quoted in Goates, 419.

44. Lee, as quoted in Goates, 408.

45. Lee, as quoted in Goates, 409.

headache and nausea. I was unable to come to the office today as I had promised ... for which I am very sorry."[46]

*

Meanwhile, President Smith's health continued its steady decline, although he attended meetings of the First Presidency and Quorum of the Twelve and delivered a brief sermon at the April 1972 general conference. But it was clear that the end was near when, on May 5, Smith blacked out while seated at the dinner table in the McConkie home. Although he rallied, he eventually succumbed two months later on July 2, 1972.[47]

Learning of Smith's death, Lee responded with emotion—surprising given the church leader's inevitable demise. "President Smith is gone," Lee gravely told his wife and daughter after Smith's son had called with the news. He then "slumped against the door frame and put his head in his arms. He kept shaking his head over and over," daughter Helen recalled. In response, Helen then reportedly stated, "Daddy dear, I guess the day has finally come that you must have thought through the years you would never be prepared for." Lee answered, "Oh, I'm afraid I'm not, I'm not." As Helen further recalled, "I had never seen him look so weak and so completely as a loss ... at that moment he was completely devastated." This prompted his wife, Joan, to assure him that he was indeed prepared.[48]

"It was only a moment, however, until he straightened up, squared his shoulders, and began to take charge," Helen continued. "The moment of weakness was gone ... and he found the resources at his command to meet the challenge of this inevitable moment."[49]

Lee suffered a major health crisis of his own just two days later on July 4. He experienced pain on his lower left side, seemingly symptomatic of a pleurisy irritation. It worsened, and he was rushed to the LDS Hospital. A series of tests revealed blood clots in his chest. Lee was compelled to remain in the hospital for twenty-four hours while medication dissolved the clots and thinned his blood.[50]

Barely recovered, Lee presided over Smith's funeral one day

---

46. Lee, as quoted in Goates, 447.
47. Gibbons, 454.
48. Helen Goates, as quoted in Goates, 454.
49. Helen Goates, as quoted in Goates, 455.
50. Goates, 458–59.

later. Lee praised his predecessor, concluding, "His death closes a chapter of history when the leadership of the Church has been in the hands of great men who were acquainted with the earliest leaders of this dispensation."[51]

*

The next day, July 7, 1972, Lee was formally set apart as eleventh president of the LDS Church. In turn, he selected as his first counselor N. Eldon Tanner and as second counselor Marion G. Romney. Tanner, a veteran general authority, had previous served as a counselor to both David O. McKay and Joseph Fielding Smith. Romney—a first cousin to national political figure George Romney—had been a long-time associate of Lee's, working with him on church welfare projects and as a fellow apostle. The two general authorities symbolized the increasingly international focus of the church: Tanner grew up in Canada, Romney was born in Mexico.[52]

Lee also called Bruce R. McConkie to the Twelve, filling the vacancy created when Romney joined the First Presidency. A member of the First Quorum of the Seventy, McConkie was well-known to the general church membership as the author of *Mormon Doctrine*, a widely used reference volume that established his reputation as a proponent of orthodox LDS beliefs and perpetuated his father-in-law's interpretations of scripture.[53]

Lee made clear his own orthodox beliefs relative to the church's direction in a wide-ranging press conference held immediately after he assumed leadership. Lee declared that "the greatest message that one in this position could give to the membership of the Church is to keep the commandments of God, for therein lies the safety of the individual."[54] When asked why the church was growing while other denominations were not, Lee stated, "The basic reason is that this Church alone holds the truth among many great churches."[55] He brushed off a question concerning the black priesthood/temple ban, stating, "For those who don't believe in modern revelation there is

---

51. Lee, as quoted in Goates, 460–61.
52. Goates, 462–64.
53. Goates, 464–66; Gibbons, 469.
54. Lee, as quoted in Goates, 465.
55. Lee, as quoted in Goates, 466.

not adequate explanation. Those who do understand stand by and wait until the Lord speaks."[56]

In response to a question concerning the unsettled state of the nation and world, Lee gloomily opined that the end times appeared near. He referenced the prophecies of church founder Joseph Smith, who was "informed by the Lord 140 years earlier, that peace would be taken from the earth and Satan would have power over his own dominion." Lee then asked ominously, "After 140 years is there any doubt to anyone that that time is here?"[57]

---

56. Lee, as quoted in Gibbons, 459.
57. Lee, as quoted in Goates, 465.

CHAPTER NINE

THE ELEVENTH CHURCH PRESIDENT
1972-73

Harold B. Lee commenced his responsibilities as LDS president with a degree of vigor and energy not seen in a church leader in decades. Throughout his brief tenure, he continued to promote correlation while overseeing church expansion both in total membership and geographic reach, facilitating Mormonism's growth into a truly international religion. Lee proved the consummate workaholic, relentlessly pushing himself despite worsening health problems. Alas, the latter proved fatal, leading to his untimely death a mere one and a half years later.

*

Barely in office as church president, Lee took two important trips abroad beginning the summer of 1972. His first journey, in late August, took him to Mexico City to preside over an area conference—the church's second outside the United States. Lee was joined by First Presidency counselors Tanner and Romney along with seven members of the Quorum of the Twelve.

By this time, Mexico boasted the largest number of church members outside the United States, numbering more than eighty-two thousand. An additional thirty-three thousand church members resided in the nearby republics of Central America.[1] This membership represented a more-than-500-percent increase over the 12,695 in 1960. Lee attributed such "vigorous growth to the influence of the Holy Ghost brooding over the land and the diligence of the missionaries and members."[2]

---

1. The figure of eighty-two thousand is in Goates, 471. Gibbons, 461, cites the higher figure of 115,000.

2. Lee, as quoted in Gibbons, 461.

A record sixteen thousand Saints gathered for the three-day conference in Mexico City's National Auditorium—making this the largest group of church members ever assembled together. Besides Lee, his counselors, and members of the Twelve, members of the Mormon Tabernacle Choir had also come to provide music.[3]

In his keynote sermon, Lee noted that "the real strength of the Church is to … be found in the total membership … in this land of Mexico and in the countries of Central America, as witnessed by the overwhelming, superabundance of the blood of Israel to be found here." At a press conference following the conference, Lee again made reference to the divinely chosen ethnicity of the Mexican people: "Every time I come to this republic I am touched by the deep faith, the dedication, and the warm friendliness of the Mexican people. They are a choice people. There is in Mexico and Central America a superabundance of the blood of Israel."[4]

Upon his return to Salt Lake City, Lee received alarming information that he was targeted for assassination at the hands of Ervil LeBaron—the leader of the schismatic Mexico-based Church of the First Born. LeBaron was rumored to be lying in wait in Salt Lake City. The Salt Lake City Police Department provided Lee welcome protection. In addition, the church's own security force accompanied Lee at all times. Lee's office suite in the Church Administration Building was equipped with electronic door safety devices designed to screen all visitors.[5]

Less than one month later, on September 12, 1972, Lee, accompanied by Joan, departed the United States for a three-week journey to Europe and the Middle East. The trip involved both overseeing church affairs and sightseeing. Joining Lee were Gordon B. Hinckley and his wife, Marjorie. Upon arriving in London, Lee tended to administrative work involving the London Temple and oversaw reorganization of the London Stake.[6]

The Lees and Hinckleys then flew to Athens. The main purpose of their visit was to secure official recognition for the church. They

---

3. Goates, 472.
4. Lee, as quoted in Goates, 474–75.
5. Goates, 476–77.
6. Gibbons, 464.

were unsuccessful. Greece bore special significance in Christian history as the Apostle Paul preached there. Mars Hill, which the Lees and Hinckleys visited, was the site of Paul's famous sermon to the pagan Greeks. Lee, in reflecting on its significance, stated, "Here then was the opening of the work among the Grecian people. As Paul began to expound the doctrine, he gave us the key as to how we all could know that Jesus was the Christ."[7]

Following that, the foursome moved on to Israel, the most important stop on their journey. Lee consulted with local officials about the possibility of the church constructing a monument on the Mount of Olives to commemorate Apostle Orson Hyde's dedicatory prayer in 1841. Also discussed was the possibility of an LDS visitors center. The Lees and Hinckleys visited a number of the sacred sites associated with Jesus: Jericho, the Sea of Galilee, Capernaum (site of the Sermon on the Mount), and Nazareth.[8]

Lee and party concluded their journey with visits to Italy and Switzerland, where they combined sightseeing with visits to church members and missionaries. In Zollikofen, just outside Bern, Lee and Hinckley visited the LDS temple, met the workers, and installed a new temple presidency. After a brief stop in New York City, the foursome returned to Salt Lake City on September 28.[9]

Lee found the entire journey enlightening and fulfilling but confessed to being "somewhat weary" at its conclusion.[10] In fact, the experience proved more exhausting than he admitted. In Greece, Lee complained of "a somewhat severe distress in his lower back, similar to the pain he suffered before President Smith's funeral" but "concealed the intensity of his pain."[11]

Lee experienced more severe health problems during his visit to the Holy Land. He confessed, "These are exhausting days. My physical Strength is at a seriously low ebb. I know something is seriously wrong. There is severe pain in my lower back and a weariness that is emphasized by a constant effort to expel mucus." Seeking relief, he received from Hinckley a healing blessing. As Lee recalled, "The

7. Lee, as quoted in Goates, 483.
8. Gibbons, 467.
9. Goates, 487–88.
10. Goates, 489.
11. As quoted in Gibbons, 465.

next morning, after a severe coughing spell ... my shortness of breath ceased, the weariness was diminished, and the back pains began to subside, and twenty-four hours later they were completely gone."[12] In further reflecting on the seriousness of this incident, he stated, "I now realize I was skirting on the brink of eternity and a miracle, in this land of even greater miracles, was extended by a merciful God who obviously was prolonging my ministry."[13]

Upon his return, Lee underwent an extensive physical examination. No outstanding residual problems were detected. This prompted Lee to note in his journal: "I feel exceptionally well, considering the pressures and experiences of the last month."[14]

*

For Lee, the October 1972 general conference bore special significance. At this gathering he was sustained as eleventh church president, which he characterized as "the greatest moment of my life."[15] He personally conducted every session throughout the three-day conclave, controlling "the tempo and spirit of the meetings." Lee's vigor and demeanor prompted his son-in-law to comment, "It had been a long time since the Church had a President who was physically able to work that hard during general conference."[16]

Lee's seemingly boundless energy was further evident in the sermons he presented. In one, he declared that the "principles and doctrines of the Church" provide "solutions to the problems that afflict the world."[17] In another, he urged church members to adhere to the laws and regulations of the federal government, going on to "bluntly denounce the actions of certain members of the Church who are in defiance of law ... refusing to pay their income taxes to the government."[18]

In yet another sermon, he described his own journey in overcoming his personal shortcomings. "Maybe it was necessary that I too must learn obedience by the things that I might have suffered—to give me experiences that were for my good, to see if I could pass

---

12. Lee, as quoted in Goates, 486.
13. Lee, as quoted in Goates, 486.
14. Lee, as quoted in Goates, 504.
15. Lee, as quoted in Goates, 497.
16. L. Brent Goates, as quoted in Goates, 503.
17. Lee, as quoted in Goates, 500.
18. Lee, as quoted in Goates, 500.

some of the various tests of mortality." He, in fact, compared his own trials to those of church founder Joseph Smith: "At times it seemed as though I too was like a rough stone rolling down from a high mountainside, being buffeted and polished, I suppose by experiences, that I too might overcome and become a polished shaft in the quiver of the Almighty."[19]

*

Anxious to reach out to young Latter-day Saints, whom he looked on as essential to the future well-being of the church, Lee attended and addressed an array of LDS youth gatherings, both within and outside of Utah.

Shortly after the October 1972 conference, Lee travelled to Mesa, Arizona, where he addressed a church youth conference of some 3,200 attendees. He then moved on to Pocatello, Idaho, where he spoke to the students of the Idaho State University Stake, proclaiming "something of a homecoming" given his Idaho roots. He next traveled to Long Beach, California, meeting a massive gathering of 14,000 young Saints.[20]

In Utah, Lee addressed two large gatherings. The first, at the University of Utah Institute of Religion, drew over 3,000 students. The second, in September 1973, was a devotional held on the BYU campus, attracting a huge audience of 23,300.[21]

The well-traveled church leader's most ambitious journey took him to Europe to preside over a three-day regional conference in Munich, West Germany. The August 1973 conference convened in Olympia Hall—which venue had accommodated the International Olympic Games a year earlier. The gathering itself was akin to the previous two regional conferences in Great Britain and Mexico. Some 14,000 church members who hailed from eight different European nations filled Olympia Hall to capacity. The addresses presented by Lee and other general authorities were translated into German, French, Italian, Spanish, and Dutch for the benefit of the diverse nationalities in attendance.[22]

---

19. Lee, as quoted in Goates, 498.
20. Gibbons, 479–80.
21. Gibbons, 480.
22. Gibbons, 486; Goates, 533–35.

Lee took note of the conference's multi-national make-up: "Although we are of different nationalities, I am reminded of the remarks of the Apostle Paul as he wrote to the Galatians in his day when he said; 'There is neither Jew nor Greek, there is neither bond nor free, there is neither male nor female; for ye are all one in Christ Jesus.'" Continuing, Lee stated, "We are neither English nor German, nor French, nor Dutch, nor Spanish, nor Italian, but we are all one as baptized members of The Church of Jesus Christ of Latter-day Saints, and also we are of Abraham's seed."[23]

In a keynote address, Lee explained the rationale behind the regional conferences: "To become acquainted with the conditions under which you live, to meet the local leaders of the Church, and to communicate with them is such a way that they might feel the unity of the purpose for which they have been called to preside in the stakes, missions, and the branches of the Church." He further noted that "we have come together in a more intimate way to strengthen the members of the Church to stand true to the covenants that they made in the waters of baptism at the time they came in as converts to the Church."[24]

Following the Munich conference, Lee, accompanied by his wife as well as Gordon Hinckley and his wife, traveled on to Vienna, Austria, and on to London, England, where they met local church leaders and missionaries. While in London, Lee took the opportunity to address yet another youth conference.[25]

*

When not traveling, Lee tended to his never-ending administrative responsibilities and matters related to correlation.

Among the most important was restructuring the Mutual Improvement Association (MIA) to make it conform to the Aaronic Priesthood Program, specifically MIA's full merger into the existing priesthood structure, a process completed in 1973. All youth programs previously under the MIA were placed under a new authority known as the Aaronic Priesthood-MIA. At the same time, a new program was inaugurated to reach out to single adults eighteen years of age and older designated the Melchizedek Priesthood-MIA

---

23. Lee, as quoted in Goates, 535.
24. Lee, as quoted in Goates, 536–37.
25. Lee, as quoted in Goates, 538–39.

(MPMIA). Assuming supervision of the MPMIA were James E. Faust, Marion D. Hanks, and L. Tom Perry.[26]

A year later, the MIA itself was abolished. Aaronic Priesthood-MIA then became simply Aaronic Priesthood, and the corollary organization for young women ages twelve to eighteen became known as Young Women. At the same time, the Melchizedek Priesthood program for LDS singles over the age of eighteen continued unaffected by the abolishment of the MIA.[27]

A second change involved tightening oversight of church expenditures. Lee called Dee Anderson to serve as full-time Church Auditor and also as executive secretary of the Church Budget Committee. Anderson, in assuming these dual positions, was expected to maintain much tighter control over church spending. At the same time, efforts were initiated to "audit" church teaching materials to make sure that such materials "attained the goals for which they were intended." Both efforts were eventually assumed by the Correlation Department under the administration of Neal A. Maxwell.

The church building program was also brought under stricter management. Under its supervision was the construction of a new Church Office Building, completed in June 1973. Located on the same city block but north of the existing Church Administration Building, the impressive twenty-eight-story structure dominated the Salt Lake City skyline as the state's tallest building. Within the structure, the church consolidated most of its administrative staff, many of whom had previously been housed in various buildings throughout the valley.[28]

Lee also pushed through important changes in the church's temple-building program. Plans were approved for the construction of a large number of smaller edifices, what was termed "stake center-sized" temples. Construction of numerous smaller temples was driven by the need to make temples easier to access for church members throughout the world. The first of these smaller temples was slated for Sao Paulo, Brazil—the first temple in South America.[29]

---

26. Gibbons, 475–77.
27. Goates, 524–27.
28. Gibbons, 484; Goates, 527.
29. Gibbons, 483; Goates, 514, 521.

The increasing internationalization of the church prompted the complete abandonment of the concept of a "central gathering place." Lee announced that, given the scattering of the Saints throughout the world, "the gathering place for the Saints was in their own home countries. Rather than move to a 'Utah Zion' they must make their homes and local stakes the places of refuge and strength by keeping the commandments of God."[30]

*

Standing in stark contradiction to Mormonism's expansion as a world region was the church's ban on black priesthood ordination and temple participation, which Lee continued to defend.

In a September 1972 newspaper interview, however, Lee appeared to soften his resistance, albeit ever so slightly, proclaiming that it was "only a matter of time before the Negro gets full status in the Church."[31] Two months later, the church authorized release of a statement through United Press International in which Lee echoed: "It's only a matter of time before the black achieves full status in the Church," adding, "We must believe in the justice of God. The black will achieve full status, we're just waiting for that time."[32]

By this time, the church in general, and BYU in particular, were no longer the target of militant demonstrations over this policy. Officials and students at the church university made a conscious effort to reach out to African Americans. In 1970, BYU student body president Brian Walton established dialogue with Black representatives from other colleges and universities.[33] BYU also launched a campaign to recruit Blacks for its athletic teams. By 1974 the school boasted Black athletes on both its football and basketball teams.[34] The school also hired an African-American professor in its College of Nursing as part of its expanded curriculum to teach students "the culture of the Negro."[35]

---

30. Lee, as quoted in Gibbons, 516.

31. *Daily Herald* (Provo, Utah), Sep. 26, 1972, 10.

32. United Press International, Statement, Nov. 16, 1972, quoted in Goates, 506.

33. For a discussion of this development, see Brian Walton, "A University's Dilemma: BYU and Blacks," *Dialogue: A Journal of Mormon Thought* 6, no. 1 (Spring 1971): 31–36; also the coverage in the *Daily Universe* (Provo, Utah), Sep. 5, 6, 9, 19, 22, 1970.

34. *Salt Lake Tribune,* Feb. 3, 1970; *Daily Herald,* Feb. 16, 1970; *San Francisco Chronicle,* Dec. 17, 1974.

35. *Daily Universe,* Dec. 4, 1970.

Within the LDS Church, efforts were made to accommodate African Americans. Room was made in the Mormon Tabernacle Choir for three black vocalists, and in 1971 a special committee headed by Gordon B. Hinckley was "charged with dealing with the Church's Negro Problem."[36]

Two active African-American Latter-day Saints spoke on behalf of the church. In his autobiography, *It's You and Me, Lord!* (1970), Alan Gerald Cherry accepted his own subordinate position. While confessing to finding it "sometimes ... frustrating," he concluded that "in the end the important thing in God's kingdom will not be who leads us there, but simply who gets there."[37] Similarly, Wynetta Willis Martin articulated her own defense of the ban in *A Black Mormon Tells Her Story*. She underscored her acceptance by including in her volume a theological defense of the ban written by John D. Hawkes.[38]

Indeed, the majority of LDS Church members accepted the ban's legitimacy. A 1972 Louis Harris Poll found that 70 percent of Utah-based Saints opposed granting blacks the priesthood. This same poll found that a significant percentage of church members believed opposition to the ban represented a "black conspiracy" to destroy the church.[39] Thus Lee's continuing affirmation of the ban represented not only his own sentiments, but those of the broader church as well.

Even so, concerned individuals within and outside of the church continued to assail the ban. The church's proposed construction of a thirty-eight-story luxury apartment building in New York City near the Lincoln Center generated opposition from Black members of the city's planning commission, who asserted that the structure represented "the poisonous myth of [black people's] alleged racial inferiority." Also opposing construction were Black residents near the site, who claimed that the building would be an "affront" to the integrated neighborhood in which it was located. Ultimately, Black residents withdrew their opposition. In return, the church

---

36. *New York Times,* Apr. 6, 1972.

37. Alan Gerald Cherry, *It's You and Me Lord!* (Provo, Utah: Trilogy Arts, 1970).

38. Wynetta Willis Martin, *Black Mormon Tells Her Story* (Salt Lake City: Hawks, 1972).

39. One third of Utah-based church members affirmed this to be the case. See *New York Times,* Apr. 6, 1972.

compensated a Black resident for his property near the site and sought to be sensitive to the needs and problems of nearby Black residents. Construction was allowed to move forward.[40]

Inside the church, Lester E. Bush Jr., an active Latter-day Saint, questioned the ban in a seminal 1973 article entitled "Mormonism's Negro Doctrine: An Historical Overview," published in *Dialogue: A Journal of Mormon Thought*. Bush undermined the official church assertion that the ban resulted from divine revelation received by Joseph Smith during the 1830s, arguing instead that it was the unfortunate byproduct of social-historical racist concepts pervasive in nineteenth-century American society. Bush argued persuasively that Brigham Young, not Joseph Smith, implemented the ban during the late 1840s, several years after Smith's death.[41]

Bush's meticulously researched, carefully written article drew heavily from his own "Compilation on the Negro in Mormonism"—a massive 400-page compilation into which, over a ten-year period, he had collected copies of First Presidency meeting minutes, Quorum of the Twelve meeting minutes, and published accounts from general authority interviews and other writings. Among the most significant items were copies of official documents from the Adam S. Bennion Papers dealing with the question.[42]

Bush obtained additional information from the recently established LDS Church Historical Department. Church Historian Leonard J. Arrington provided essential help and encouragement. Bush shared the results of his research, in particular his "Compendium on the Negro in Mormonism," with Joseph Anderson, Arrington's supervisor, and with Apostle Boyd K. Packer. Bush hoped to convince church leaders to lift the ban based on his conclusion that the ban had not originated with Joseph Smith.[43]

---

40. *New York Times*, Oct. 12, 1972; *New York Times*, Dec. 15, 1972; *New York Times*, Dec.21, 1972.

41. Lester E. Bush Jr., "Mormonism's Negro Doctrine: An Historical Overview," *Dialogue: A Journal of Mormon Thought* 8, no. 1 (Spring 1973): 11–63.

42. Lester E. Bush, Jr., "Compilation on the Negro in Mormonism," copy in the Newell G. Bringhurst Papers, Manuscripts Division, J. Willard Marriott Library, University of Utah, Salt Lake City.

43. Lester E. Bush discussed the process and its consequences in his "Writing 'Mormonism's Negro Doctrine: An Historical Overview (1973): Context and Reflections, 1998," *Journal of Mormon History* 25 no.1 (Spring 1999): 229–71.

Instead, Bush found himself under attack from ranking members of the church hierarchy. Upon reading Bush's work, Lee lamented, "Unfortunately this study quoted from the minutes of the Quorum of the Twelve that had gotten into the papers of [Apostle Adam S. Bennion who was] unwise enough to let it [sic] go to [the] BYU library."[44] Prior to the publication of Bush's article, Packer sought, but failed, to convince Bush not to publish it.[45]

The article's publication generated condemnation from church leaders. Particularly outspoken were Apostles Bruce R. McConkie and Mark E. Petersen. McConkie dismissed Bush's article as "crap;" Petersen pushed, unsuccessfully, for Bush's excommunication from the church.[46]

Church leaders vigorously defended the doctrinal legitimacy of the ban, Lee authorizing the republication of his 1945 essay "Youth of a Noble Birthright," which affirmed the ban as divinely sanctioned. The essay, reproduced exactly as written eighteen years earlier, was included in a 1973 church-sanctioned volume entitled *Decisions for Successful Living.*[47]

In addition, Lee found himself confronting the ban on a personal level. A young LDS woman, Rula Jorgensen Sargent, had recently married Carlos Sargent, an African-American non-member. The young woman's mother, Margaret Jorgensen, the daughter of Hugh B. Brown, whose family Lee knew on a first-name basis, sought Lee's counsel in a September 1973 letter.

In her letter, Jorgensen acknowledged her family's dismay upon first learning of Rula's involvement with Sargent, urging her to end

---

44. As quoted in *Confessions of a Mormon Historian: The Diaries of Leonard J. Arrington, 1971–1997,* ed. Gary James Bergera, 3 vols. (Salt Lake City: Signature Books, 2019), 1:423. Lee further stated, "Ours is a private archive and not a public one, and that we do not wish confidential materials to be made generally available." The Bennion materials were removed from the BYU Library and placed in the LDS Church Archives where access was restricted.

45. As recalled by Bush in "Writing 'Mormonism's Negro Doctrine,'" 254–59.

46. As recalled by Bush in "Writing 'Mormonism's Negro Doctrine,'" 266–67. Apostle Petersen persisted in his efforts to have Bush excommunicated. Some ten years later, in March 1983, Petersen instructed Washington, DC Stake president J. Willard Marriott to "take some appropriate action" against Bush, whose publication Petersen criticized "very harshly." Ultimately, Marriott opted not to excommunicate Bush.

47. Harold B. Lee, *Decisions for Successful Living* (Salt Lake City: Deseret Book Co., 1973), 161–69.

the relationship. But Rula persisted. As Margaret and the rest of the family got to know Sargent, they were soon won over by his demeanor and moral character. Rula's grandfather Hugh Brown upon learning of their engagement, asked Margaret, "Can he [Carlos] make her [Rula] happy?" When his daughter replied yes, Brown simply stated, "Give Rula my love, tell her as long as they love each other they will work things out." Thus, the young couple married with the approval of the family.[48]

However, Jorgensen was perplexed by their new son-in-law's reluctance to become a Latter-day Saint. Informing Lee of this, she stated: "Carlos is eager to join the Church but he is deeply disturbed, bewildered, and depressed because as he tells his wife, 'I'm cursed—I'm of the seed of Cain—I have the Devil in me, Therefore I am not worthy to be a member of the Church of Jesus Christ.'" She further informed Lee that her son-in-law was "not rationalizing" and added, "He has no bad habits to give up—he is simply overcome by a feeling of inferiority. To him, he has been dealt the ultimate blow—being rejected by the Lord, himself!"[49]

Lee, in responding to this "very serious problem," asked, "I am not sure just what you had in mind in writing me." He ignored the anguish and instead lectured Jorgensen about the ban itself: "Now, Margaret, this is something that the Lord has not made known to anyone. The early Brethren have said that if those who were presently denied the Priesthood were to be true and faithful as Church members, the time would come when they would receive the blessings of the Priesthood. Until that time comes, we have no answer. But ... the Priesthood is not given to those who are restricted for reasons that are known only to the Lord."[50]

Lee's response is revealing for what it said and what it omitted. Clearly stated was Lee's affirmation of the ban. The letter also affirmed Lee's long-standing opposition to interracial marriage. Finally, Lee's letter showed that he had no intention of lifting the ban.

*

48. Margaret Brown Jorgensen to Harold B. Lee, Sep. 12, 1973, courtesy of Reid Moon.
49. Jorgensen to Lee.
50. Lee to Margaret Brown Jorgensen, Oct. 1, 1973, courtesy of Reid Moon.

Meanwhile, Lee moved forward with preparations for the October 1973 general conference—the last over which he would preside.

Through his own conference addresses, Lee expressed his concerns about issues affecting the church faithful. In one sermon he admonished single priesthood holders over age twenty-five, accusing them of "shirking their responsibilities as husbands and fathers." He further stated, "Marriage is not a man-made institution. It is of God. It is honorable, and no man who is of marriageable age is living his religion who remains single."[51]

In a second address, Lee expressed alarm over "the fearful wave of marriage dissolution" evident not just in the larger society but within the church itself. He lamented: "One of the most painful things that I have as a responsibility is to have to work through the flood of recommendations for cancellations of [temple marriage] sealings of those who have been married in the temple. It is frightening ... much of it stems from one of the greatest of all sins, next to murder, the sin of adultery, that is running rampant throughout the Church."[52]

In a third talk, Lee expressed concern about unsettled conditions outside the church. The period 1972–73 proved particularly traumatic given the ongoing Watergate scandal, which divided Americans, combined with unrest in Latin America and the Middle East—the latter region thrust into all-out war, pitting Israel against its Arab neighbors. Lee tended to describe such events in apocalyptic terms, affirming that the "moving hand of the Lord" was present "in the affairs of the nations of the world today. We see the signs of our times as foretold by the prophets and by the Master, himself." Lee rhetorically asked: "Where is there safety in the world today?" In answer, he continued: "Safety can't be won by tanks and guns and airplanes and atomic bombs. There is only one place of safety and that is within the realm of the power of the Almighty God that he gives to those who keep the commandments and listen to his voice, as he spoke through the channels that he has ordained for that purpose."[53]

In his concluding sermon, Lee stated, "We have never had a conference where there has been so much direction, instruction, so much

---

51. Lee, as quoted in Goates, 543–44.
52. Lee, as quoted in Goates, 544.
53. Lee, as quoted in Goates, 545–46.

admonition, where the problems have been defined and also the solution to the problem has been suggested. ... If it were not for the assurance that the Lord is near to us, guiding and directing," he continued, "the burden would be almost beyond my strength, but I know that He is there, and that He can be appealed to." Lee ended: "Peace be with you, not in the peace that comes from the legislation in the halls of congress, but in the peace that comes ... by overcoming all the things of the world" and following "the brethren" in strict obedience.[54]

*

Meanwhile, Lee tended to the needs and concerns of his immediate family. Joan proved an ideal companion, although she could not completely fill the void left by Fern. Much to Lee's relief, Joan remained in good health throughout their years together, avoiding the health-related problems that had plagued his first wife. Joan, moreover, both complemented and enhanced Lee's ability to relate and interact with young Latter-day Saints given her background as an educator.

Lee took pride in his eight grandchildren—seven of whom were boys, thus providing consolation for not having a son of his own. At the same time, Lee manifested concern for the four children of his deceased daughter Maureen, whose death had deeply affected her family. Although her husband ultimately remarried and fathered four additional children, the second marriage eventually failed, much to the distress of his concerned father-in-law.

Lee's own health remained a concern. In March 1973, he underwent treatment to cure a chronic lung infection. He was admitted to the hospital where, under the direction of his personal physician, a bronchoscopy was performed. Afterwards, Lee went through an intensive physical therapy program that lasted several weeks. The condition was further treated through a regimen of heavy medication.[55]

*

Health concerns notwithstanding, Lee kept up a rapid pace for the remainder of 1973.

In late October, he and Joan traveled to Rexburg, Idaho, where he addressed students at Ricks College. In a surprisingly partisan

54. Lee, as quoted in Goates, 546–47.
55. Goates, 575.

presentation to some 5,000 students, Lee referenced the ongoing Watergate scandal. "We are living in a time of great crisis. The country is torn with scandal and with criticism, with faultfinding and condemnation. It is an easy thing to climb on the bandwagon and join the hotheads in condemnation, little realizing that when they do, they are not just tearing down a man, they are tearing down a nation, and they are striking at the underpinnings of one of the greatest nations in the world." Clearly defending the besieged president Richard M. Nixon, Lee continued: "We should not be concerned with finding out what is wrong with America but we should be finding out what is right about America and should be speaking optimistically and enthusiastically about America."[56]

In early November, Lee delivered a very different message to members of Salt Lake City's Federal Heights Ward—Joan's and his home ward. In an impromptu presentation, he asserted the existence of Satan and his adverse effects on humanity. "I say this to you by way of warning, that I know that the adversary lives and operates in the affairs of man. And he is determined to cause a downfall of men. If he can't get to us, he will try to get to those closest to us, for he is in a mighty battle with the work of the Savior. And I must tell these words of warning. So, keep close to the Lord."[57]

The following month, on December 9, Lee addressed members of the city's Cannon Stake, over which his older brother, Perry, presided as stake president. At age seventy-eight, Perry Lee was the oldest stake president in the church. Cannon Stake was once part of Pioneer Stake, over which Harold Lee had once presided. In his presentation, Lee referred to the current uncertain times, urging listeners to store food, clothing, and fuel against shortages that were occurring throughout the country. "Some have not listened," he warned, "and now it may be too late."[58]

Four days later, on December 13, Lee delivered what was to be his last major address to seven thousand church employees and their partners assembled for an annual Christmas gathering in the Salt Lake Tabernacle. Again, he alluded to uncertain times, asking "Do

---

56. Lee, as quoted in Goates, 558.
57. Lee, as quoted in Goates, 564.
58. Lee, as quoted in Goates, 567.

all of you who are close to us here ... listen to the Brethren who ... urge you to put aside in storage for at least one year, food, fuel, clothing? Have you done that today?"[59]

In one final public appearance on December 18 at an annual Christmas party for employees of the Beneficial Life Insurance Company, Lee arrived late. After apologizing, he simply remarked, "I would not have come out tonight for anyone else except you. I am so weary that I would have stayed home. But I felt strongly compelled to be here in support of you and Beneficial Life."[60]

*

Given Lee's schedule of activities throughout the last three months of 1973, his death on December 26 came as a complete shock to all who knew and interacted with him.

On the morning of December 26, Lee awoke feeling fatigued, despite having slept ten hours. His personal physician was summoned to the family residence where he conducted a complete physical examination. Upon discovering rales in Lee's lungs—an abnormal sound characterized by clicking or rattling—he had Lee admitted to the hospital for further tests. After being examined by a specialist, Lee was found to be anemic, due in part to blood loss from coughing earlier that morning. He was also found to have lung failure from chronic bronchitis. Further examination discovered a more critical problem: heart failure. Lee was immediately placed on oxygen. His condition worsened and he soon went into cardiac arrest. All efforts to revive him failed. He was pronounced dead at 8:58 p.m.—six hours after his admission to the hospital.[61]

Son-in-law L. Brent Goates, a hospital administrator, recalled feelings of intense denial mixed with forlorn hope as he witnessed his father-in-law's passing: "I still waited for the miracle. He had been saved through three other hospitalizations. He was at the pinnacle of his performance in Church leadership. The Kingdom needed him. No one could take his place. We knew the Lord knew that and we had exercised our faith and priesthood. Now when was the Lord going to come to our rescue? He could send angels to help.

---

59. Lee, as quoted in Goates, 567.
60. Lee, as quoted in Goates, 568.
61. Goates, 575–80.

I knew it must come soon, but I waited, expectantly. It could come at any moment now. But ... it never came."[62]

Church officials closest to Lee likewise expressed feelings of disbelief. N. Eldon Tanner stated: "President Lee's passing is a great shock to all of us, the greatest shock I've experienced in my life, and the sadness cannot be adequately expressed." A second general authority, William Grant Bangerter, stated, "It was expected when he [Lee] became President he would preside for twenty years or more ... It was the first time since the death of the Prophet Joseph Smith when the president had died before it was time for him to die."[63] Church members, in fact, had grown accustomed to watching presidents of the church live long lives. Lee was the youngest president to die since Joseph Smith.[64]

In its tribute to Lee, the Council of the Twelve adopted a resolution stating: "He was a prophet ... who spoke and acted with unswerving courage and boldness in applying the teachings of the Savior to the challenges and problems of these turbulent times. Indeed, it could be said of him, as it had been said of his predecessor, Brigham Young: 'He was a lion of the Lord.'"[65]

Tributes also came from outside the LDS community. Rabbi Abner Bergman of Salt Lake City's Congregation Kol Ami stated, "I knew President Lee in an official capacity as well as personally, and always found him to be a paragon of warmth, kindness, and personal integrity ... I will miss him."[66] James F. Oates Jr., chair of the board of directors of Equitable Life Assurance Society, on which Lee had served, characterized his associate as "enormously effective, not only in the business aspects of this great enterprise, but also as a spiritual leader."[67] Religious leader Norman Vincent Peale, pastor of the Collegiate Reformed Church in New York City, commented: "I was shocked at the news at the passing of my good friend, President Harold B. Lee. I admired him tremendously. He was one of the most enlightened and creative religious leaders in the world. A giant has

---

62. L. Brent Goates, as quoted in Goates, 580–81.
63. William Grant Bangerter, as quoted in Goates, 584.
64. Goates, 584.
65. Resolution of the Council of Twelve Apostles, as quoted in Goates, 586.
66. Abner Bergman, as quoted in Goates, 588.
67. James F. Oates Jr., as quoted in Goates, 587.

fallen."[68] And from sitting US president Richard Nixon came the following: "Mrs. Nixon and I were deeply saddened to learn of the sudden death of Harold B. Lee … I knew him as a warm and generous friend whose counsel and prayers I valued greatly."[69]

Following a public viewing, in which Lee's body lay in state in the marble rotunda of the Church Administration Building, funeral services were conducted on December 30 in the Salt Lake Tabernacle. Among the speakers paying tribute was First Counselor Tanner who summed up the character of the man: "Our beloved President was always working as though he had a deadline to meet, and that he must meet it running a high speed. He never thought of his own comfort or convenience. We urged him on many occasions to take a little respite, to relax and rest, but he seemed never to be concerned about himself."[70] Second counselor Marion G. Romney stated: "Never in my experience has the Church been better organized and better administered than under [President Lee's] great leadership. He truly was one of the greatest prophets who have walked the earth."[71]

And finally, Spencer W. Kimball, destined to succeed Lee as church president, expressed his own feelings of shock: "President Lee has gone. I never thought it could happen … I have not been ambitious. I am four years older than Brother Lee (to the exact day, March 28). I have expected that I would go long before he would go. My heart cries out to him and for him." Kimball further characterized Lee as "great, noble" and "giant of a man."[72]

Lee was laid to rest in the Salt Lake City Cemetery amid a downpour of rain following the funeral. In beginning his dedicatory prayer, L. Brent Goates stated: "It is not unfitting that the heavens should weep today, because we, the Church membership worldwide, weep too—for ourselves—at the sudden passing of President Lee."[73]

---

68. Norman Vincent Peale, as quoted in Goates, 587.
69. Richard M. Nixon, as quoted in Goates, 586.
70. N. Eldon Tanner, as quoted in Goates, 597–98.
71. Marion G. Romney, as quoted in Goates, 598.
72. Spencer W. Kimball, as quoted in Goates, 593, 597.
73. L. Brent Goates, as quoted in Goates, 603.

PERSONALITY, TEACHINGS, LEGACY

To all who knew and interacted with Harold B. Lee, the dynamic church leader projected a commanding presence reflective of an assertive personality, sharp intelligence, and deep spirituality. All this belied his modest 5' 8" frame, accentuated by a handsome appearance, thick hair, and "a kind face."[1]

Marion G. Romney, a close friend who served as Lee's second counselor in his First Presidency, judged him as among "the most powerful men in modern Israel [the church]."[2] Romney praised Lee's "ministry [as] characterized by an uncommon originality and daring. ... We who sat with him daily, were frequently startled by the scope of his vision and the depth of his understanding."[3] In summing up Lee's religious certitude, Romney further stated, "To him, his Heavenly Father was a senior partner, daily giving him guidance. Few indeed have had contacts with heaven as direct and regular as he did. He was more like the Prophet Joseph Smith than other man I've ever associated with. He seemed to get the inspiration of the Lord spontaneously."[4]

General authority Neal A. Maxwell characterized Lee as "personally kind, and yet very tough-minded intellectually." "Because he knew the gospel to be true," Maxwell added, "he was fearlessly

---

1. As recalled by Elaine Cannon, a former Young Women's general president, in L. Brent Goates, ed., *He Changed My Life: Personal Experiences with Harold B. Lee* (Salt Lake City: Bookcraft, 1988), 208.

2. Marion G. Romney, as quoted in Goates, *He Changed My Life*, 23.

3. Marion G. Romney, as quoted in Harold B. Lee, *Ye Are the Light of the World: Selected Sermons and Writings* (Salt Lake City: Deseret Book Co., 1974), x.

4. Marion G. Romney, as quoted in Goates, *He Changed My Life*, 24.

confrontive," and thus able "to deal with institutional and personal feedback from a position of security."[5] Lee also "had a reputation among his brethren for being both intimidating and demanding."[6] Marion Romney was blunter about the subject, "Listen, if he [Lee] wants to tell you something, he'll tell you. He'll take the hide off you if it isn't going well."[7]

Such behavior was reflective of Lee's so-called "nemesis," his "hot temper."[8] Romney recalled a particular incident when Lee administered a "tongue lashing" to a member of the welfare committee, but then dismissed his action as a mere "burst of truth." Shocked by Lee's outburst, Romney hoped "such would not 'burst upon him.'"[9] Also taking note of Lee's volatile personality was Wendell J. Ashton, director of the church's Public Communications Department, who stated that "President Lee could be very tough, if the situation called for it. ... Some people felt that he expressed too much sharpness at times."[10] Neal Maxwell observed Lee giving "reproof to others," adding that such behavior was often followed by an "outpouring of redemptive affection" intended "to help the individuals who had been reproved and counseled."[11]

At the same time, Lee projected a deep compassion for others. In the words of Marion Romney, "He understood and loved the underprivileged"—most evident perhaps in his supervision of the Church Welfare Program.[12] Such empathy was further evident in Lee's interaction with young Latter-day Saints: "He loved the youth with a divine compassion" and, at the same time, "sorrowed over the rebellious and unrepentant and rejoiced over the returning prodigal."[13] Further evidence of Lee's empathy was his willingness to personally mingle and interact with rank-and-file church members.

---

5. As quoted in Goates, *He Changed My Life*, 239.
6. As quoted in Bruce C. Hafen, *A Disciple's Life: The Biography of Neal A. Maxwell* (Salt Lake City: Deseret Book Co., 2002), 326.
7. As quoted in Hafen, *A Disciple's Life*, 326.
8. As asserted in Blaine M. Yorgason, *Humble Servant, Spiritual Giant: The Story of Harold B. Lee* (Ogden, Utah: Living Scriptures, 2001), 247.
9. As quoted in Goates, *Harold B. Lee*, 213.
10. As quoted in Goates, *He Changed My Life*, 240.
11. As quoted in Goates, *He Changed My Life*, 88.
12. As noted by Marion G. Romney, in Lee, *Ye Are the Light of the World*, vii.
13. Marion G. Romney, as quoted in Lee, *Ye Are the Light of the World*, viii.

Paul H. Dunn, a one-time member of the First Quorum of the Seventy, proclaimed Lee "a compassionate person," always "sensitive to his audience" and not "so hurried or harassed that he couldn't take a minute to sincerely greet and visit with a new friend." Indeed, Lee possessed a "rare genius" for identifying with such individuals.[14] Personal evidence of Lee's empathy was his frank admission: "I realized that before I could be worthy of the high place to which I had been called, I must love and forgive every soul that walked the earth."[15]

Another hallmark was Lee's obsession with continually engaging in church service. "His work was never-ending," recalled Glen L. Rudd, a one-time member of the First Quorum of the Seventy. Lee was "always the slave to a schedule of appointments and demands, rarely having time to do anything that would be pleasurable to him. … It mattered little how he felt or whether he was well enough to do the job. The job had to be done, and he had to do it."[16] Thus, Lee "did not engage in recreation as such"—his sole advocation evidently being gardening and yard work.[17]

Lee's relentless work schedule took a toll on him physically. Rudd observed that although Lee presented himself as "a strong, vigorous man," he was plagued by "headaches, fatigue, and more than his share of minor and major irritations and sicknesses." But he "was never one to complain or to seek sympathy," going about "his daily tasks in an uncomplaining, quiet manner." Indeed, Lee's "closest companions in the Council of the Twelve were surprised to learn of his chronic ailments" following his death.[18]

Early in Lee's ministry, a close family friend, John K. Edmunds, questioned Lee about his workaholism. Edmunds, alarmed over Lee's facial "marks of strain and fatigue," recalled: "The tired eyes and the obvious drain on his energy caused me to say, 'You look very tired, Brother Lee. This must have been a very hard assignment for you.'" Lee confessed that "it was," going on to "relate some of the problems that he had confronted." This prompted Edmunds to

---

14. Paul H. Dunn, as quoted in Goates, *He Changed My Life*, 221–22, 224.

15. Harold B. Lee, general conference address, Oct. 1946, as quoted in Lee, *Ye Are the Light of the World*, xi.

16. As quoted in Goates, *He Changed My Life*, 19, 21.

17. As noted by Yorgason, *Humble Servant*, 205.

18. As quoted in Goates, *He Changed My Life*, 19–20.

suggest to Lee "that he ease up a little in his ... work." Otherwise, Edmunds warned, "your health might break under the strain." Lee rejected his friend's advice, reaffirming his determination to "giving my full strength and energy to my calling."[19]

*

Lee saw his role as a teacher to be of primary importance, promoting orthodox, conservative, scripturally based LDS doctrines.[20] Lee "was always teaching," noted Apostle Boyd K. Packer, an associate and protégé. "If one had the sensitivity to listen, his [Lee's] lessons were always substantive, never trivial, always helpful."[21]

Lee reached out to the youth of the church through a series of twenty-four weekly radio sermons, collectively published in 1945 as *Youth and the Church*. In the volume's foreword, fellow apostle Ezra Taft Benson praised the sermons for their "refreshing ... straight-forwardness" in addressing "the problems of youth in the light of the eternal principles and present world conditions. ... Both young and old will find in this volume safe answers to perplexing problems of companionship, courtship, marriage, home-building, [and] everyday choices of right or wrong."[22]

Twenty-eight years later, Lee oversaw the republication of his twenty-four sermons in an updated, expanded volume under the title *Decisions for Successful Living*. In a new foreword, Gordon B. Hinckley praised the volume for its "divine wisdom, spoken in various dispensations and preserved and 'brought forth by the gift and power of God.'" Hinckley extolled its sermons for "truths of timeless value expressed in a contemporary setting."[23] The volume's sermons dealt with "subjects that concern every soul in the never-ending

---

19. As quoted in Goates, *He Changed My Life*, 111–12.

20. Many, if not a majority, found their way into various church publications throughout Lee's tenure as a general authority. A significant sampling of these was published in the following: Lee, *Youth and the Church* (1945); Lee, *Decisions for Successful Living* (1973); Lee, *Ye Are the Light of the World* (1974); Lee, *Stand Ye in Holy Places* (1974); Clyde J. Williams, ed., *The Teachings of Harold B. Lee* (Salt Lake City: Bookcraft, 1996); and *Teachings of the Presidents of the Church: Harold B. Lee* (Salt Lake City: Church of Jesus Christ of Latter-day Saints, 2000).

21. As quoted in Goates, *He Changed My Life*, 41.

22. Ezra Taft Benson, as quoted in Lee, *Youth and the Church*, viii.

23. Gordon B. Hinckley, as quoted in Lee, *Decisions for Successful Living*, vii.

contest between truth and error, righteousness and wickedness."[24] In the opening essay, Lee urged Latter-day Saints to "keep the commandments taught herein, search the scriptures, pray always, and be obedient, and eternal success will be yours."[25]

Decisions for Successful Living included four new sermons. In "Strengthening the Home," Lee expressed alarm over changing social mores during the 1960s. Lee believed that such forces threatened the "traditional family," specifically the "sacred relationships of husband and wife, of parents and their children." In noting the ever-higher divorce rate, he urged husbands and wives to "be true" to one another, thus avoiding "the Great sin of Sodom and Gomorrah … a sin second only in seriousness to the sin of murder."[26] He vigorously denounced "the grievous sin of homosexuality which seems to be gaining momentum with social acceptance in the Babylon of today's world," contending that such "sexual perversions" must be vigorously opposed "through every lawful means which can be employed."[27]

In "Fortifying One's Self for the Future," Lee pointed to other "frightening events" of the 1960s, specifically racial violence resulting from urban unrest—this representing a "maelstrom of mob psychology." All of this he attributed to the "potent … insidious forces of evil mastered by the ruler of darkness of that world." Lee admonished his followers to "watch and pray, be on guard always, lest Satan tempt you and you be led captive by him."[28] The church leader characterized "life as a member of the Church of Jesus Christ of Latter-day Saints [akin to] crossing a swinging bridge suspended between the points of birth by baptism and death into eternal life over a turbulent stream of wickedness and sin."[29]

A selection of Lee's other teachings appeared in two subsequent volumes: *Stand Ye in Holy Places* and *Ye Are the Light of the World*, both published in 1974. In the foreword to *Stand Ye in Holy Places*,

---

24. Lee, *Decisions for Successful Living*, ix.

25. Lee, *Decisions for Successful Living*, 2.

26. Lee, *Decisions for Successful Living*, 243, 246. In condemning "the Great sin of Sodom and Gomorrah" Lee was referring to adultery rather than homosexuality—the context in which the expression is usually used. Lee's meaning is evident when read in the entire sermon's context.

27. Lee, *Decisions for Successful Living*, 250.

28. Lee, *Decisions for Successful Living*, 221–22.

29. Lee, *Decisions for Successful Living*, 227, 234.

Spencer W. Kimball noted that when Lee spoke "of the trumpet giving a certain sound, he [was] calling men to action, to worthiness, to cleanliness." Kimball added that Lee's counsel was "firm, yet loving, and given with forthrightness, to help men gain an eternal perspective and to live their lives as taught by the Lord."[30]

A major theme in Lee's published sermons was obedience to divine authority. In "Make Our Lord and Master Your Friend," Lee warned Latter-day Saints that to "escape from the devastations when God's judgements descend upon the wicked," they must walk "'in obedience to the commandments' which ... include honesty, moral purity, together with all the laws of the celestial kingdom."[31] Likewise, in "Time to Prepare to Meet God," he warned that every mortal was offered the choice of either "liberty and eternal life though obedience to the laws of God, or captivity and death as to spiritual things because of disobedience." All humankind, he promised, could "be saved by obedience to the laws and ordinances of the Gospel."[32] In "How to Receive a Blessing from God," Lee stated that "when we obtain any blessings from God, it is by obedience to that law upon which it is predicated."[33]

Lee further emphasized obedience in "The Iron Rod," a hard-hitting essay in which he emphatically declared that "the rod of iron" as revealed to Book of Mormon prophet Lehi was "the word of God." The iron rod, he proclaimed, was "a safe guide along the straight path on the way to eternal life, amidst the strange and devious roadways that would eventually lead to destruction and to the ruin of all that is 'virtuous, lovely, or of good report.'"[34] Lee ridiculed church members who, "in their smugness," ask: "Do the revelations of God give us a handrail to the Kingdom of God, as the Lord's messenger to

---

30. Spencer W. Kimball, as quoted in Lee, *Stand Ye in Holy Places*, iii–iv.

31. Originally presented as an October 1968 general conference address and reprinted in Lee, *Stand Ye in Holy Places*, 24.

32. Originally presented as an October 1970 general conference address and reprinted in Lee, *Stand Ye in Holy Places*, 235, 236. In his latter statement, Lee was directly quoting from the Third Article of Faith.

33. Originally presented as a 1966 Mutual Improvement Association address and reprinted in Lee, *Stand Ye in Holy Places*, 241. In this latter statement, Lee was quoting from the Doctrine and Covenants 131:21–22.

34. Originally presented as an October 1971 general conference address and reprinted in Lee, *Stand Ye in Holy Places*, 351.

Lehi, or merely a compass?" Lee compared such individuals to the "scoffers in Lehi's vision—standing aloof and seemingly inclined to hold in derision the faithful who chose to accept Church authorities as God's special witnesses." Lee further denounced "those in the Church who speak of themselves as liberals" and "read by the lamp of their own conceit. ... A liberal in the Church," he scoffed, "is merely one who does not have a testimony."[35]

Lee expressed conservative views both doctrinally and politically, condemning what he saw as alarming trends in American society at large. In an essay entitled "Have Faith in America," Lee lamented: "We are living in an age when we have seen black called white and white called black, and sin called good and good called sin." He condemned two recent US Supreme Court decisions. One was the controversial *Roe v. Wade* decision legalizing abortion under certain conditions—a practice he denounced as "contrary to all of the teachings of the scriptures [and] one of the most heinous sins." The second was *Engel v. Vitale,* which Lee assailed as mandating "the eradication of prayer and Bible reading from our public school system."[36] In general, Lee lamented the "immorality ... gripping the nation," pointing to "pornography ... being distributed all over the country and affecting the lives of our young people." He condemned the "sexual revolution, as it is called, where sex in every horrible form of perversion is being portrayed on the public screen, over television, and on the stage."[37]

The essay, however, ended on a positive note, with Lee asserting that "hundreds of thousands" of citizens are flocking to those denominations that oppose such developments, specifically pointing to the LDS Church, which seemed to be growing at an unprecedented rate. "I think this speaks well for the intelligence of the American people. ... Men may fail in this country ... but this nation, founded on principles laid down by men whom God has raised up will never fail."[38]

Lee's other teachings were featured in *Ye Are the Light of the World,* likewise published in 1974—all of which further underscored Lee's

---

35. Lee, *Stand Ye in Holy Places,* 352, 353–55.
36. Lee, *Stand Ye in Holy Places,* 349.
37. Lee, *Stand Ye in Holy Places,* 349–50.
38. Lee, *Stand Ye in Holy Places,* 350–51.

orthodox, conservative beliefs. In "Preparing Our Youth," Lee noted that "the future of the Church is bound up in our youth," and thus "we must do a better job of preparing them than we are now doing." "An unloved child, a child who has not known discipline, work, nor responsibility, will often yield to satanic substitutes for happiness—drugs, sexual experimentation, and rebellion."[39]

Lee stressed the importance of the family, focusing specifically on the role of women through a series of six essays contained in a special section entitled "Women's Glorious Purpose." In each of the six, he affirmed women's so-called "traditional role." All of this represented a vigorous rebuttal to the women's liberation movement and the pending Equal Rights Amendment—both of which he considered as further assaults on the integrity of the traditional nuclear family.

In the first essay, entitled "Women's Glorious Purpose," Lee declared, "The responsibility of the mother" is "to put the father at the head of the house." Further emphasizing this point, he wrote, "Wives, never, never, let [your husband] feel that you don't understand him. Put father at the head of the house."[40] Similarly, in the second essay, "Maintain Your Place as a Woman," Lee stated: "To be a wife is one of your greatest responsibilities—true companion, a helpmeet to your husband." He further asserted, "No man can live piously, or die righteously without a wife. ... Only in holy wedlock for time and eternity ... can the man and woman attain to the highest privilege in the celestial world."[41]

In "Three Phases of Motherhood," Lee extolled the virtues of motherhood. "There are three phases of motherhood" he declared, "first, the bearing of children; next, the rearing of children; and third—and perhaps the most important of all—the loving of children. ... If you would reform the world from error and vice, begin by enlisting the mothers. The future of society is in the hands of mothers."[42]

"The best school of discipline," he continued, "is the home, for

---

39. Originally published in *Ensign*, Mar. 1971, and reprinted in Lee, *Ye Are the Light of the World*, 63, 64, 66.

40. As reprinted from the *Relief Society Magazine*, Jan. 1968, in Lee, *Ye Are the Light of the World*, 277.

41. As reprinted from *Ensign*, Feb. 1972, in Lee, *Ye Are the Light of the World*, 283–84.

42. Sermon presented at an April 1970 Primary conference and reprinted in Lee, *Ye Are the Light of the World*, 293, 294.

threat was being contained by eliminating intellectual inquiry from Church education."[55] Indeed, Correlation, although innovative in its conception and bold execution, reflected Lee's basic conservatism, both theological and political, along with his "preference for centralized and standardized leadership and control [and] stress upon obedience, especially to the living prophet, and ... suspicion of scholars and intellectuals."[56]

Such conservative ideals were perpetuated in a second significant way, through Lee's mentoring of those men who followed him into the Quorum of the Twelve. The most prominent of these were Spencer W. Kimball, Ezra Taft Benson, Howard W. Hunter, Gordon B. Hinckley, and Thomas S. Monson—each of whom, in turn, succeeded Lee as church president. Among the other important general authorities whom Lee trained were N. Eldon Tanner, Marion G. Romney, and Boyd K. Packer—each of whom influenced the subsequent course of church doctrine and practice.

Harold B. Lee was "the right man in the right place at the right time" who, in the words of LDS historian and intellectual Richard D. Poll, himself the target of some of Lee's pointed criticisms, "will surely be remembered as one of the ten most influential General Authorities in the History of the Church."[57]

55. These are the words of Armand L. Mauss in *The Angel and the Beehive: The Mormon Struggle with Assimilation* (Urbana: University of Illinois Press, 1994), 82.

56. Mauss in *The Angel and the Beehive*, 81.

57. As quoted in Richard D. Poll, "The Swearing Elders: Some Reflections," *Sunstone*, Dec. 1985, 17.

---

family life is God's own method of training the young, and homes are largely what mothers make them." Lee related the role of his own mother in helping him to avoid the pitfalls of his own youthful foolishness: "I was one of those ... careless teenage boys, warned by [my] mother of certain impending danger that I flicked away as not being meaningful, only to find within a matter of weeks that the danger of what she warned me was a fact. I should have gone back to her and thanked her for it, but I guess she knew; and today I express my thanks, for, except for that counsel, I might not have been worthy of the place to which I am now called."[43]

In "For All Eternity, If Not for Time," Lee sought both to console and reassure those faithful LDS women, who, though married, did not bear children; he also tried to comfort single, unmarried women. To married, childless women, Lee stated that "although not privileged to bear children in mortality [they] may through sacred ordinances in holy temples on earth, in the Lord's own time, be sealed to a worthy husband; and in this sealing by divine authority, if acceptable to both, could in the world beyond this one permit a holy union in eternal wedlock, with the promise of posterity beyond the grave." Likewise, unmarried single women, "who have not yet accepted a proposal of marriage, if you make yourselves worthy and ready to go to the house of the Lord and have faith in the sacred principle of celestial marriage for eternity, even though the privilege of marriage does not come to you in mortality, the Lord will reward you in due time and no blessing will be denied you."[44]

"The Role of Women in Building the Kingdom" likewise underscored the importance of traditional marriage and motherhood for Latter-day Saint women. "The role of women in the great plan of salvation" involves making "a career of motherhood."[45] The final essay in this section, "Reap the Rewards of Beautiful Women," focused on the young women of the church. "Within the heart of every lovely girl there is a desire for companionship with a young man. This is not an evil impulse. It comes from our Heavenly Father" just

43. Lee, *Ye Are the Light of the World*, 295, 294.

44. As reprinted from *Relief Society Magazine*, Oct. 1968, in Lee, *Ye Are the Light of the World*, 307, 308.

45. Sermon presented at September 1966 Relief Society conference and published in Lee, *Ye Are the Light of the World*, 311, 315, 319.

as "there is in the breast of every fine young man a desire for companionship with a lovely young woman." But Lee warned: "Because these impulses are very strong, Satan tries to inflame them beyond their natural bounds; [Satan] tries to put into the mind of the young man to become ungentlemanly … he tries to get the young woman to dress in an immodest way or to invite with unholy invitation her young companion. Satan knows that thereby these impulses might be inflamed beyond their natural bounds."[46]

Lee's teachings on a wide range of topics reflected a conservative philosophy involving all aspects of doctrine and practice. Such was clearly underscored in his 1969 sermon "That Thy Light May Be a Standard unto the Nations." Specifically, he stated, "In the midst of social unrest and so-called minority group disturbances, there are some disturbing tendencies among us today. I mention only three. … First there is the dangerous temptation to compromise Church doctrines and standards in order to satisfy worldly pleasures, to change things that, in the final analysis, only God can change," adding, "that tendency is clearly among some of our leaders in the Church."[47] Lee was clearly referring to ongoing efforts to lift the church's controversial ban on black priesthood ordination and admission to the temple, then being spearheaded behind the scenes by First Presidency counselor Hugh B. Brown.

A second of Lee's concerns involved efforts by "some in our church schools and seminaries and institutes to challenge, under the guise of so-called academic freedom, the doctrinal purity and Church standards." Lee condemned those Latter-day Saints who encouraged "dissent against Church institutions and divinely appointed authority. Faith was never built by providing the dissenters with a forum to criticize the Church, its institutions, and its authority. … The Church doesn't need anything new except as the Lord reveals his will through revelation."[48]

*

Notwithstanding his brief tenure as church president, Harold B.

Lee's legacy was profound, in both the short and long ter[m] "was unusually gifted with the ability to administer large sca[le] grams—to devise means of solving massive problems in a p[ractical] way."[49] Correlation was, without question, Lee's greatest co[ntribu]tion. Such reform proved essential given rapid church grow[th] concurrent geographic expansion.

Correlation, or the "The Lee Revolution" as it was calle[d] resented "a major step in the quest for a modern church tha[t] enforce a sense of orthodoxy and obedience and keep the w[orld at] bay." "With a new corporate structure, a centralized bureau[cracy,] revitalized priesthood and other modern amenities … the [church] was poised for another burst of expansion."[50] Correlation, i[t] helped to accelerate the process of carrying the message of Mo[rmon]ism abroad. As Lee himself stated, "No longer might this chu[rch be] thought of as the 'Utah Church' or as an 'American church,' [the] membership of the Church is now distributed all over the ea[rth.] Her boundaries are being enlarged, her stakes are being str[ength]ened."[51] At the same time, Correlation caused "the experie[nce of] being a Mormon from ward to ward and country to country [to be]come increasingly uniform."[52] Lee's "broadened perspective re[sulted] from a life of administrative responsibility and lifelong experie[nce] developing and executing programs to benefit people," noted [Leon]ard J. Arrington, the dean of Mormon historians.[53]

At the same time, Correlation "tightened the screws on [po]tentially errant membership." "Centralized control, the maj[or goal] of the correlation movement, caused many [church] memb[ers to] question whether there was any room for tolerance and autono[my.] While Correlation was originally intended to "eliminate du[plication] and inefficient programs," it ultimately produced "a standa[rdized] and sanitized instructional curriculum [in which the] intell[ectual]

46. Originally delivered as an address at the 1972 Mexico City area conference and reprinted in Lee, *Ye Are the Light of the World*, 322, 323.

47. Originally delivered as a June 29, 1969 MIA conference address, and reprinted in Lee, *Ye Are the Light of the World*, 3–10.

48. Lee, *Ye Are the Light of the World*, 7, 8.

49. As noted by Leonard J. Arrington in "Harold B. Lee," in Arrington, [ed.,] *Presidents of the Church* (Salt Lake City: Deseret Book Co., 1986), 344.

50. As it was called in Robert Gottlieb and Peter Wiley, *America's Saints: The [Rise of] Mormon Power* (New York: G. P. Putnam's Sons, 1984), 62.

51. Harold B. Lee, Apr. 1973 general conference address, in *Ensign*, July 197[3,]

52. These are Matthew Bowman's words in *The Mormon People: The Makin[g of an] American Faith* (New York: Random House, 2012), 195.

53. As noted by Arrington in "Harold B. Lee," 345.

54. As noted by Bowman in *The Mormon People*, 195.

family life is God's own method of training the young, and homes are largely what mothers make them." Lee related the role of his own mother in helping him to avoid the pitfalls of his own youthful foolishness: "I was one of those ... careless teenage boys, warned by [my] mother of certain impending danger that I flicked away as not being meaningful, only to find within a matter of weeks that the danger of what she warned me was a fact. I should have gone back to her and thanked her for it, but I guess she knew; and today I express my thanks, for, except for that counsel, I might not have been worthy of the place to which I am now called."[43]

In "For All Eternity, If Not for Time," Lee sought both to console and reassure those faithful LDS women, who, though married, did not bear children; he also tried to comfort single, unmarried women. To married, childless women, Lee stated that "although not privileged to bear children in mortality [they] may through sacred ordinances in holy temples on earth, in the Lord's own time, be sealed to a worthy husband; and in this sealing by divine authority, if acceptable to both, could in the world beyond this one permit a holy union in eternal wedlock, with the promise of posterity beyond the grave." Likewise, unmarried single women, "who have not yet accepted a proposal of marriage, if you make yourselves worthy and ready to go to the house of the Lord and have faith in the sacred principle of celestial marriage for eternity, even though the privilege of marriage does not come to you in mortality, the Lord will reward you in due time and no blessing will be denied you."[44]

"The Role of Women in Building the Kingdom" likewise underscored the importance of traditional marriage and motherhood for Latter-day Saint women. "The role of women in the great plan of salvation" involves making "a career of motherhood."[45] The final essay in this section, "Reap the Rewards of Beautiful Women," focused on the young women of the church. "Within the heart of every lovely girl there is a desire for companionship with a young man. This is not an evil impulse. It comes from our Heavenly Father" just

---

43. Lee, *Ye Are the Light of the World*, 295, 294.

44. As reprinted from *Relief Society Magazine*, Oct. 1968, in Lee, *Ye Are the Light of the World*, 307, 308.

45. Sermon presented at September 1966 Relief Society conference and published in Lee, *Ye Are the Light of the World*, 311, 315, 319.

as "there is in the breast of every fine young man a desire for companionship with a lovely young woman." But Lee warned: "Because these impulses are very strong, Satan tries to inflame them beyond their natural bounds; [Satan] tries to put into the mind of the young man to become ungentlemanly ... he tries to get the young woman to dress in an immodest way or to invite with unholy invitation her young companion. Satan knows that thereby these impulses might be inflamed beyond their natural bounds."[46]

Lee's teachings on a wide range of topics reflected a conservative philosophy involving all aspects of doctrine and practice. Such was clearly underscored in his 1969 sermon "That Thy Light May Be a Standard unto the Nations." Specifically, he stated, "In the midst of social unrest and so-called minority group disturbances, there are some disturbing tendencies among us today. I mention only three. ... First there is the dangerous temptation to compromise Church doctrines and standards in order to satisfy worldly pleasures, to change things that, in the final analysis, only God can change," adding, "that tendency is clearly among some of our leaders in the Church."[47] Lee was clearly referring to ongoing efforts to lift the church's controversial ban on black priesthood ordination and admission to the temple, then being spearheaded behind the scenes by First Presidency counselor Hugh B. Brown.

A second of Lee's concerns involved efforts by "some in our church schools and seminaries and institutes to challenge, under the guise of so-called academic freedom, the doctrinal purity and Church standards." Lee condemned those Latter-day Saints who encouraged "dissent against Church institutions and divinely appointed authority. Faith was never built by providing the dissenters with a forum to criticize the Church, its institutions, and its authority. ... The Church doesn't need anything new except as the Lord reveals his will through revelation."[48]

*

Notwithstanding his brief tenure as church president, Harold B.

46. Originally delivered as an address at the 1972 Mexico City area conference and reprinted in Lee, *Ye Are the Light of the World*, 322, 323.

47. Originally delivered as a June 29, 1969 MIA conference address, and reprinted in Lee, *Ye Are the Light of the World*, 3–10.

48. Lee, *Ye Are the Light of the World*, 7, 8.

Lee's legacy was profound, in both the short and long term. Lee "was unusually gifted with the ability to administer large scale programs—to devise means of solving massive problems in a personal way."[49] Correlation was, without question, Lee's greatest contribution. Such reform proved essential given rapid church growth and concurrent geographic expansion.

Correlation, or the "The Lee Revolution" as it was called, represented "a major step in the quest for a modern church that could enforce a sense of orthodoxy and obedience and keep the world at bay." "With a new corporate structure, a centralized bureaucracy, a revitalized priesthood and other modern amenities ... the church was poised for another burst of expansion."[50] Correlation, in turn, helped to accelerate the process of carrying the message of Mormonism abroad. As Lee himself stated, "No longer might this church be thought of as the 'Utah Church' or as an 'American church,' but the membership of the Church is now distributed all over the earth. ... Her boundaries are being enlarged, her stakes are being strengthened."[51] At the same time, Correlation caused "the experience of being a Mormon from ward to ward and country to country to become increasingly uniform."[52] Lee's "broadened perspective resulted from a life of administrative responsibility and lifelong experience in developing and executing programs to benefit people," noted Leonard J. Arrington, the dean of Mormon historians.[53]

At the same time, Correlation "tightened the screws on a potentially errant membership." "Centralized control, the major aim of the correlation movement, caused many [church] members to question whether there was any room for tolerance and autonomy."[54] While Correlation was originally intended to "eliminate duplicate and inefficient programs," it ultimately produced "a standardized and sanitized instructional curriculum [in which the] intellectual

49. As noted by Leonard J. Arrington in "Harold B. Lee," in Arrington, ed., *The Presidents of the Church* (Salt Lake City: Deseret Book Co., 1986), 344.

50. As it was called in Robert Gottlieb and Peter Wiley, *America's Saints: The Rise of Mormon Power* (New York: G. P. Putnam's Sons, 1984), 62.

51. Harold B. Lee, Apr. 1973 general conference address, in *Ensign*, July 1973, 4.

52. These are Matthew Bowman's words in *The Mormon People: The Making of an American Faith* (New York: Random House, 2012), 195.

53. As noted by Arrington in "Harold B. Lee," 345.

54. As noted by Bowman in *The Mormon People*, 195.

threat was being contained by eliminating intellectual inquiry from Church education."[55] Indeed, Correlation, although innovative in its conception and bold execution, reflected Lee's basic conservatism, both theological and political, along with his "preference for centralized and standardized leadership and control [and] stress upon obedience, especially to the living prophet, and ... suspicion of scholars and intellectuals."[56]

Such conservative ideals were perpetuated in a second significant way, through Lee's mentoring of those men who followed him into the Quorum of the Twelve. The most prominent of these were Spencer W. Kimball, Ezra Taft Benson, Howard W. Hunter, Gordon B. Hinckley, and Thomas S. Monson—each of whom, in turn, succeeded Lee as church president. Among the other important general authorities whom Lee trained were N. Eldon Tanner, Marion G. Romney, and Boyd K. Packer—each of whom influenced the subsequent course of church doctrine and practice.

Harold B. Lee was "the right man in the right place at the right time" who, in the words of LDS historian and intellectual Richard D. Poll, himself the target of some of Lee's pointed criticisms, "will surely be remembered as one of the ten most influential General Authorities in the History of the Church."[57]

---

55. These are the words of Armand L. Mauss in *The Angel and the Beehive: The Mormon Struggle with Assimilation* (Urbana: University of Illinois Press, 1994), 82.

56. Mauss in *The Angel and the Beehive*, 81.

57. As quoted in Richard D. Poll, "The Swearing Elders: Some Reflections," *Sunstone*, Dec. 1985, 17.